THE MUST-HAVE AIR FRYER COOKBOOK

The Complete Air Fryer Recipes Cookbook with Mouthwatering Recipes for Beginners & Advanced Users

By

Clara Miles

Francis Michael

ISBN: 978-1-952504-59-4

COPYRIGHT © 2020 by Clara Miles

All rights reserved. This book is copyright protected and it's for personal use only. Without the prior written permission of the publisher, no part of this publication should be reproduced, distributed, or transmitted in any form or by any means, including photocopying, recording, or other electronic or mechanical methods.

This book is sold with the idea that the author is not needed to render accounting, officially permitted, or otherwise, qualified services. It's recommended to seek for the services of a legal or professional, a practiced individual in the profession if advice is needed.

DISCLAIMER

The information written in this publication is geared for educational and entertainment purposes only. Concerted efforts have been made towards providing accurate, up to date and reliable complete information. The information in this book is true and complete to the best of our knowledge.

Neither the publisher nor the author takes any responsibility for any possible consequences of reading or enjoying the recipes in this book. The author and publisher disclaim any liability in connection with the use of information contained in this book. Under no circumstance will any legal responsibility or blame be apportioned against the author or publisher for any reparation, damages, or monetary loss due to the information herein, either directly or indirectly.

Table of Contents

INTRODUCTION 10
- Benefits of Cooking with Your Air Fryer 10
- How to Make Use of Your Air Fryer 12
- How to Effectively Clean Your Air Fryer 14
- Effective Ways to Maintain Your Air Fryer 15
- Air Fryer Frequently Asked Questions and Answers 16
- Air Fryer Cooking Charts 18

AIR FRYER BREAKFAST RECIPES 21
- Breakfast Frittata 21
- Sweet Potato Hash 22
- Pumpkin Muffins 23
- Sausage Breakfast Casserole 24
- Breakfast Sandwich 25
- Baked Apple 26
- Breakfast Pockets 27
- French Toast Sticks 28
- Breakfast Toad-in-the-Hole Tarts 29
- Cranberry Pecan Muffins 30
- Frozen Mozzarella Sticks 31
- Frozen French Fries 32
- Spicy Sweet Potato Wedges 33
- Spam Fritters 34
- Peanut Butter and Jelly Air Fried Doughnuts 35
- Flourless Crunchy Onion Rings 37
- Breakfast Potatoes 38
- Breaded Dill Pickle Chips 39
- Blueberry Lemon Muffin 40

Pitta Pizza 41

Rosemary Roast Potatoes 42

Mini Cheese Scones 43

Cheesy Homemade Garlic Bread 44

AIR FRYER MAIN MEALS 45

Sweet Potato Fries 45

Roasted Brussels Sprouts 46

Parmesan Truffle Oil Fries 47

Kale Chips 48

Rich Fruit Scones 49

Gyro Meatballs 50

Spanish Spicy Potatoes 51

Sausage Rolls 52

Cheese & Onion Pasties 53

Chewy Granola Bars 54

Roasted Swede 55

Garlic Parsley Potatoes 56

Seasoned Asparagus 57

Rock Buns 58

AIR FRYER POULTRY RECIPES 59

Chicken Schnitzel 59

Chicken Tikka 60

Mini Turkey Pies 61

KFC Chicken Strips 62

Chicken Wrapped In Bacon 63

Lemon Pepper Chicken 64

Buffalo Chicken Legs 65

Frozen Chicken Wings 66

Chicken Fried Rice 67

Honey Garlic Chicken Wings 68

Crispy Chicken Nuggets 69

Buttermilk Chicken 70

Chinese Chicken Wings 71

KFC Popcorn Chicken 72

Turkey Spring Rolls 73

AIR FRYER FISH & SEAFOOD RECIPES 74

Lemon Garlic Shrimp 74

Fried Catfish 75

Air Fryer Salmon 76

Crispy Coconut Prawns 77

Shrimp Scampi 78

Homemade Cajun Breakfast Sausage 79

Coconut Shrimp with Spicy Marmalade Sauce 80

Crumbed Fish 81

Bang Bang Fried Shrimp 82

Fish and Chips 83

Garlic Lime Shrimp Kabobs 84

Bacon Wrapped Filet Mignon 85

Cajun Salmon 86

Coconut Shrimp 87

Honey-Glazed Salmon 88

Cajun Shrimp 89

Tomato Mayonnaise Shrimp 90

AIR FRYER BEEF & PORK RECIPES 91

Pork Chops 91
Beef Empanadas 92
Stromboli 93
Roasted Stuffed Peppers 94
Rib Eye Steak 95
Pork Taquitos 96
Beef Hotpot 97
Country Fried Steak 98
Pork Rinds 99
Taco Bell Crunch Wraps 100

AIR FRYER EGG RECIPES 101
Egg Rolls 101
Puffed Egg Tarts 102
Easy Breakfast Sandwich 103
Avocado Egg Boat 104
Hard Boiled Eggs 105
Baked Eggs 106
Breakfast Soufflé 107
Scrambled Eggs 108
Frozen Egg Rolls 109
Easy Omelette 110
Chicken Egg Rolls 111
Baked Eggs in Bread Bowls 112
Bacon & Eggs 113
Cheese and Veggie Egg Cups 114
Easy Full English 115

AIR FRYER SIDE DISH RECIPES 116

Pizza Hut Bread Sticks 116

Sloppy Joes Stuffed Cheese Scones 117

Garlic Potatoes 118

Courgette Fritters 119

Air Fryer Croutons... 120

Cheese Pull Apart Bread 121

Stuffed Garlic Mushrooms 122

Sage & Onion Stuffing Balls 123

Pigs In Blankets 124

AIR FRYER BURGER RECIPES 125

Double Cheese Burger 125

Bunless Burgers 126

Veggie Burgers 127

Turkey Burgers 128

Falafel Burger.. 129

Lentil Burgers.. 130

Hamburgers 131

Lamb Burgers 132

Mediterranean Burgers... 133

Juicy Lucy Cheese Burger 134

AIR FREYR VEGAN & VEGETARIAN RECIPES 135

Vegetable Samosas 135

Buffalo Cauliflower 136

Potato Chips 137

Sticky Mushroom Rice 138

Veggie Bake Cakes 139

Cauliflower Chickpea Tacos 140

Fried Ravioli 141

Mediterranean Vegetables 142

Spicy Cauliflower Stir-Fry 143

Cheesy Potato Wedges 144

Vegan Potato Latkes 145

Thai Veggie Bites 146

AIR FRYER APPETIZER RECIPES 148

Roasted Parsnips 148

Monte Cristo Sandwich 149

Cinnamon Toast 150

Spicy Dill Pickle Fries 151

Stuffed Mushrooms with Sour Cream 152

Mozzarella Sticks 153

Bacon-Cheddar Stuffed Potato Skins 155

Tomato Basil Scallops 156

Grilled Cheese Sandwich 157

Buffalo-Ranch Chickpeas 158

French Toast Soldiers 159

Greasy Home Fried Potatoes 160

Blooming Onion 161

Sweet Potato Tots 162

Zucchini Gratin 163

Fried Pickles 164

AIR FRYER DESSERT RECIPES 165

Fried Banana S'mores 165

Apple Dumplings 166

Peach and Blueberry Cobbler 167

Stuffed Apple Pies 169

Banana Sandwich 170

Homemade Chocolate Cake 171

Air Fryer Donuts 172

Flaky Buttermilk Biscuits 173

Apple Cinnamon Empanadas 174

Mini Cherry and Cheese Streusel Tartlets 175

Sugared Dough Dippers with Chocolate Amaretto Sauce 176

Steak French Fries 177

Apple Fries with Caramel Cream Dip 178

Homemade Vanilla Bean Cake 179

INTRODUCTION

Benefits of Cooking with Your Air Fryer

There are lots of benefits one gets using an air fryer to cook. Although there are other cooking methods but the benefits and comfort derived from cooking with an air fryer are overwhelming. The benefits are listed below:

1. **Universality:**

The air fryer has a universal feature which means it is capable of doing a multipurpose function you may want to do with it. Some people used microwave oven to fry but I tell you, the air fryer is comparable to microwave oven. It can fry chicken to the best of your taste. It may interest you to know that the air fryer can bake cake easily. Yes!!! It can bake cake very easily. Other food that you can cook with air fryer includes: all kinds of frozen foods, veggies, casserole, fish, meat etc.

One interesting feature of the air fryer is dividable basket. This helps you to cook different kinds of foods at the same time. Other extra features that could be found in some fryers include grill or baking pan, cooking rack, rotisserie rack etc. Air fryer has different sizes with different accessories that you can buy.

2. **Saves Space:**

This unit is usually easy to store and move when necessary. Unlike coffee maker, the size of air fryer is similar to it. The unit also has the ability to replace a cooker like toaster oven. Yes!!! It can replace undoubtedly. Those that are living in a small apartment with a small kitchen will benefit a lot from this unit because the size is handy and does not consume enough space in the kitchen.

3. **Gives Healthy Cooking:**

Despite the fact that the appliance can fry food with or without oil, it gives healthy cooking. It can be used to cook frozen fires, wings and onions. At the end of the cooking, you will still have crispy result even without using oil while frying. The unit can also be used to make breaded zucchini and gives you an overwhelming result.

4. **Very Easy to Clean:**

After cooking a big meal, the next thing you have to do is cleaning the appliance. There is no much work here and does not take enough of your time washing it after cooking. The air fryer only requires you to clean just a pan and a basket. Cooked food goes off to your plate. They do not get stuck to the grill pan because of the nonstick coated parts.

5. **More Efficient in Energy:**

The air fryer does not unnecessarily cause more heat inside your kitchen. When you are cooking using the air fryer, you will still feel the comfort of your room because will it not make your room to be too hot.

6. Cooks Meal Faster:

Due to their portability, the air fryer cooks meal faster within the specified time. Unlike a microwave which takes about 30 minutes to preheat, the air fryer can take about 10-13 minutes to come to temperature. Approximately, frozen fry can take up to about 13–15 minutes to be well cooked using the air fryer compared to a microwave oven which may take up to 40-45 minutes for the fries to be well cooked. This shows how faster the air fryer cooks. This unit is best for those who are in a hurry to prepare a meal.

7. Simple to Use:

Some people do not like cooking appliances that are so cumbersome to operate. The air fryer only needs just 4 simple steps to start cooking which includes: selecting the temperature, setting the cooking time, adding food and shaking it after sometimes while still cooking. The baskets make shaking of your food simple and fast as well.

How to Make Use of Your Air Fryer

The uniqueness of Air fryers lies in the fact that they can be used to deliver any fries with just a single drop of oil. This is possible with the following steps:

1. **Set the Cooking Temperature:**

Setting the temperature is always the first thing you need to do when using the air fryer. What you need to do is to convert a recipe with a suggested temperature for any deep frying using a local or traditional oven. Just reduce the temperature of air fryer by 25°F. This will give you the same result as that of a traditional oven.

For instance, if a given recipe requires the temperature to be heated up to 400°F in a traditional oven, cook at 375°F for air fryer. The rule is pertinent because air on circulation makes the cooking heat to be more intense compared to a local cooking method. Before you start cooking with the air fryer, do not forget to preheat your air fryer.

2. **Add the Ingredients with Little Oil:**

The air fryer requires that you put one or two tablespoons of oil before you put the ingredients. However, there are foods that contain lots of fat (like meatballs), it needs no extra cooking oil.

It is recommended that if you are cooking any food that has already been coated with flour and you want to get the food turn to golden brown, spray the air fryer basket first with a light cooking oil and putting the food into the air fryer basket in layers. In the other hand, there are foods that can be cooked without putting extra oil.

3. **Place the Food on the Air Fryer Basket:**

For you to be able to cook foods that are coated with flour, you place them in layer(s). There are some air fryer models that have two layer racks. Such racks that allows for two layers will enable you to cook two different things at the same time but will require a longer cooking time and will result in food that are not well cooked, that is why it is advisable to shake the air fryer after 3 or 4 minutes of the cooking time to ensure the food is cooked properly.

4. **Check Regularly for Doneness:**

Foods cook with the air fryer usually cooks faster than the foods cook with a traditional method. This is so because the temperature of the air fryer environment is being maintained consistently by the circulating air.

It should be noted that if you already know the recipe for a particular food and you wants to convert it to cook in the air fryer, you have to be checking the food regularly for doneness. For instance if the cooking time for a given food is 20 minutes, you have to check the food after 15 minutes and then cook again for the remaining 5 minutes.

5. **Frozen French Fries Possible to Make:**

Yes! It's true. Frozen French fries could be successfully cooked using the air fryer. The impressive fact about this is that it does not necessarily require that you put oil into the air fryer before you can cook the fries. This is usually cooked at 350ºF for 15 minutes. Do not fail to shake one or two times while cooking. You may add salt to it if needed and also top with preferred garnish.

How to Effectively Clean Your Air Fryer

Air fryers are always clean. Cooking of food locally could sometimes be boring. Pans get dirty, coating board gets greasy, utensils get grimy, and other things around the fryer gets dirty. Air fryer cooking basket is closed inside the unit. This helps to avoid some drops of oil, grease, fat into the oil pan below. However, it is necessary to clean the air fryer all the time after use. In order to clean the unit, follow these simple steps:

1. If the air fryer was plugged to the wall socket, unplug it and allow it cool down.

2. Clean the outside with a wet cloth.

3. All the air fryer's components that are removable are dishwasher safe. You just need to put them into a dishwasher if you want to wash them using dishwasher. For other components put a dishwashing soap into warm water, wash the cooking tray, pan, and basket.

4. Use hot water to clean the inside of the air fryer with hot water and a cloth.

5. Check the air fryer's food basket if there is any food stuck above the heating element. Clean it.

6. After washing the cooking basket, tray and pan, ensure to allow them dry before fixing them back to the unit.

Effective Ways to Maintain Your Air Fryer

Air fryer needs proper maintenance to extend its durability and prevent it from damaging. The maintenance steps include the following:

1. Before you start cooking make sure the air fryer is placed on a level surface. Place it in upright position.

2. Before you start cooking make sure the air fryer is clean and free from any dirt. Check inside of the unit for debris if it has been a long time you used the unit. Check the pan and basket and clean them if you found some dust.

3. Before any use, check the basket and pan for any damage. Replace any damaged parts by contacting the manufacturer.

4. Check the cables before you start using the unit. Replace any damaged cable in order to avoid unexpected injuries. This can lead to death so ensure the cables are in good condition all the time.

5. Air fryers need at least 4 inches of space behind them and 4 inches of space above them to properly vent steam and hot air while cooking and be free from unnecessary overheating. Avoid keeping the unit at close range with another appliance. Do not keep it close to the wall.

Air Fryer Frequently Asked Questions and Answers

These are the six most commonly asked questions for every beginner.

1. **What kind of food can I cook in the Air fryer?**

This is the first question that thrills the minds of beginners. Indeed there is no food you cannot cook with the air fryer. You can cook any kinds of fries, snacks, chicken, meat, and also bake cake with the air fryer. Vegetables which have to be cooked (such as carrot and broccoli) are less suitable to prepare in an Air fryer. Other vegetables can be cooked with the air fryer. A lot of people are now using the air fryer to cook frozen foods

Moreover, anything you can cook with your oven is possible to cook with your air fryer faster than the oven. If there is no preparation and cooking time available on the food packaging for air fryer, you don't have to panic. Just subtract 25ºF from the one of the oven. For instance if the oven cooking temperature is 200ºF for 20 minutes, cook in the air fryer at 175º F for 12 minutes.

2. **Where can I purchase the best Air fryer?**

Any new air fryer you purchase is the best product. Some people like to purchase a second hand product. There is no problem with that but you need to be careful so that you don't buy fake product.

3. **How much food can I cook per batch in an Air fryer?**

Air fryer has different types of models and the amount of food to be cooked per batch depends on the model of the air fryer. All the cooking baskets have their recommended amount of food you can put at a time. Do not overload the basket. If you are to put big large amount of food, it depends on the food as explained below:

Snacks: Avoid putting snacks that is more than 500 gram (18 oz.) into the cooking pan or basket at the same time. You only need to cover the bottom of the cooking basket to achieve a good result. Do not fail to shake the basket half way during cooking time so that the snacks will be properly cooked.

Rising products: This kind of food is somehow difficult to determine quantity per batch due to its rising ability. When it starts rising do not allow it to reach the level of the heat element. If that happens, it has negative impact on your air fryer.

Potatoes or any fries: You can fill the basket up to the brim level. Do not forget that large quantities could result in uneven doneness of the fries. For an improved result, you need to shake the cooking pan or basket about 2-3 times before the cooking time is completed.

Stuffed vegetables and delicate foods: These are food that you need to take them out after cooking. You have to keep enough space to enable you take them out again after cooking. Generally, to determine the amount of food to be loaded at a given batch sometimes should depend on your own judgment and base on your experience.

4. **Is it mandatory to preheat my Air Fryer?**

It depends on the type of food you are preparing. Some foods require preheating the air fryer while some foods do not require preheating the air fryer. If no preheating is done, you might have to leave your meal in slightly longer. Some foods are required to be placed in the Air fryer before it is pre-heated. For instance cooking an egg need the air fryer to be preheated. Usually, preheating the air fryer does not need much time, just 2-3 minutes. Some air fryers beep when the air fryer come up to temperature. When the air fryer is preheated, fill the basket and set the timer to the required cooking time.

5. **Does food cooked in an Air fryer taste sweet?**

The best answer to this question is for you to try it yourself. A trial will convince you. Air fryer has the capacity to make your food look crispy on the outside and makes the inside soft. Indeed food cooked with an air fryer has a delicious taste. Air fryer is good for cooking snacks, French fries, chicken etc. Applying a little oil on the food (like chicken) will enhance the effect of your air fryer. Air fryer does not necessarily require oil to cook your food but will still give you a delicious taste.

6. **What are the important accessories the Air fryer needs?**

Most air fryers are delivered to the standard that can enable you to cook all kinds of foods. With this, you do not need extra accessories. If you still insist on getting extra accessories, you could consider buying a grill pan designed for the Air fryer. This ensures that the product is ready even faster and makes grilling meat, fish and vegetables even easier. There are other accessories which are often used with the Air fryer. They include the following:

Grill Mat: This is used to keep the basket clean. A grill mat is however easier to clean than the Air fryer basket. The grill mat can also be used in the same way as the flame distributor in order to prevent some light food items come against the heating element.

Flame Distributor: Air fryer flame distributor could be handy. The flame divider is usually used to cover the food. The heating element which is located above the basket will not have any splashes. The flame distributor also helps to prevent pine nuts, crumbs and other light food items blowing up against the heating element. A commonly used flame distributor for Air fryer XL is the Handy flame distributor of Blokker.

Bakes: There are some dishes that require being prepared in a casserole. Place the casserole out of the bottom of the pan, but in the basket. This will maintain the air circulation in the air fryer.

Air Fryer Cooking Charts

Chicken:

Chicken	Temperature (º F)	Time (Min)
Wings (2 lbs.)	400º F	12
Whole Chicken (6.5 lbs.)	360º F	75
Breast, bone in (1.25 lbs.)	370º F	25
Breasts, boneless (4 oz.)	380º F	12
Drumsticks (2.5 lbs.)	370º F	20
Thighs, bone in (2 lbs.)	380º F	22
Thighs, boneless (1.5 lbs.)	380º F	18 - 20
Legs, bone in (1.75 lbs.)	380º F	30
Tenders	360º F	8 - 10

Beef:

Beef	Temperature (º F)	Time (Min)
Meatballs (1-inch)	380º F	7
Meatballs (3-inch)	380º F	10
Burger (4 oz.)	370º F	16 - 20
Fillet Mignon (8 oz.)	400º F	18
Flank Steak (1.5 lbs.)	400º F	12
London Broil (2 lbs.)	400º F	20 - 28
Beef Eye Round Roast (4 lbs.)	390º F	45 - 55
Sirloin Steaks (1-inch, 12 oz.)	400º F	9 - 14
Ribeye, bone in (1-inch, 8 oz.)	400º F	10 - 15

Fish & Seafoods:

Fish & Seafoods	Temperature (º F)	Time (Min)
Shrimp	400º F	5
Tune Steaks	400º F	7 - 10
Scallops	400º F	5 - 7
Fish Fillet (1-inch, 8 oz.)	400º F	10
Swordfish Steak	400º F	10
Calamari (8 oz.)	400º F	4
Salmon, Fillet (6 oz.)	380º F	12

Pork & Lamb

Pork & Lamb	Temperature (°F)	Time (Min)
Sausages	380° F	15
Rack of Lamb (1.5 – 2 lbs.)	380° F	22
Loin (2 lbs.)	360° F	55
Bacon (thick cut)	400° F	6 - 10
Lamb Loin Chops (1-inch thick)	400° F	8 - 10
Pork Chops, bone in (1-inch, 6.5 oz.)	400° F	12
Tenderloin (1 lb.)	370° F	15
Bacon (regular)	400° F	5 - 7

Frozen Foods

Frozen Foods	Temperature (°F)	Time (Min)
Fish Sticks (10 oz.)	400° F	10
Breaded Shrimp	400° F	9
Onion Rings (12 oz.)	400° F	8
Chicken Nuggets (12 oz.)	400° F	10
Pot Stickers (10 oz.)	400° F	8
Fish Fillets (1-inch, 10 oz.)	400° F	14
Mozzarella Sticks (11 oz.)	400° F	8
Thick French Fries (17 oz.)	400° F	18
Thin French Fries (20 oz.)	400° F	14

Vegetables

Vegetables	Temperature (°F)	Time (Min)
Onions (pearl)	400° F	10
Mushrooms (sliced ¼-inch)	400° F	5
Zucchini (1/2-inch sticks)	400° F	12
Tomatoes (halved)	350° F	10
Kale Leaves	250° F	12
Tomatoes (cherry)	400° F	4
Green Beans	400° F	5
Fennel (quartered)	370° F	15
Sweet Potato (baked)	380° F	30 - 35
Eggplant (1/2-inch cubes)	400° F	15
Corn on the cob	390° F	6

Squash (1/2-inch chunks)	400° F	12
Potatoes (baked whole)	400° F	40
Cauliflower (florets)	400° F	12
Potatoes (1-inch chunks)	400° F	12
Potatoes (small baby, 1.5 lbs.)	400° F	15
Carrots (sliced ½-inch)	380° F	15
Peppers (1-inch chunks)	400° F	15
Brussels Sprouts (halved)	380° F	15
Parsnips (1/2- inch chunks)	380° F	15
Broccoli (florets)	400° F	6
Beets (whole)	400° F	40
Asparagus (sliced 1-inch)	400° F	5

AIR FRYER BREAKFAST RECIPES

Breakfast Frittata

Preparation time: 15 minutes

Cook time: 20 minutes

Total time: 35 minutes

Ingredients:

- ¼ lb. of breakfast sausage, fully cooked and crumbled
- 4 eggs, beaten
- ½ cup of shredded Cheddar-Monterey Jack cheese blend
- 2 tbsp. of red bell pepper, diced
- 1 green onion, chopped
- 1 pinch cayenne pepper, optional
- Cooking spray

Cooking Instructions:

1. In a medium bowl, combine together the sausage, eggs, Cheddar-Monterey Jack cheese, bell pepper and onion.

2. Add the cayenne and give everything a good mix to combine.

3. Preheat your Air Fryer to 360°F (180° C). Spray a nonstick cake pan with cooking spray.

4. Add the egg mixture in the prepared cake pan and place into the Air Fryer.

5. Cook for about 18 to 20 minutes or until frittata is set.

6. Serve and enjoy!

Sweet Potato Hash

Servings: 6

Preparation time: 10 minutes

Cook time: 15 minutes

Total time: 25 minutes

Ingredients:

- 2 large sweet potato, cut into small cubes
- 2 slices of bacon, cut into bite pieces
- 2 tbsp. of olive oil
- 1 tbsp. of smoked paprika
- 1 tsp. of sea salt
- 1 tsp. of ground black pepper
- 1 tsp. of dried dill weed

Cooking Instructions:

1. Preheat your Air Fryer to 400°F (200°C).

2. In a medium bowl, add together the sweet potato, bacon, olive oil, paprika, salt, pepper, and dill.

3. Add the mixture into the preheated Air Fryer.

4. Cook for about 12 to 16 minutes. Stir after 10 minutes and cook until crispy and browned.

5. Serve and enjoy!

Pumpkin Muffins

Preparation time: 2 minutes

Cook time: 15 minutes

Total time: 17 minutes

Servings: 12

Ingredients:

- 1 cup of pumpkin puree
- 2 cups of gluten free oats
- ½ cup of honey
- 2 eggs, lightly beaten
- 1 teaspoon of coconut butter
- 1 tablespoon of cocoa nibs
- 1 tablespoon of vanilla essence
- 1 teaspoon of nutmeg

Cooking Instructions:

1. Add all of the ingredients in the blender and blend everything until smooth.
2. Add the muffin mix into little muffin cases, and spread it over 12 separate ones.
3. Add into your Air Fryer and cook for about 15 minutes at 180°C.
4. Serve and enjoy!

Sausage Breakfast Casserole

Preparation time: 10 minutes

Cook time: 20 minutes

Total time: 30 minutes

Servings: 4

Ingredients:

- 1 pound of hash browns
- 1 pound of ground breakfast sausage
- 1 green bell pepper, diced
- 1 red bell pepper, diced
- 1 yellow bell pepper, diced
- ¼ cup of sweet onion, diced
- 4 large eggs

Cooking Instructions:

1. Place a piece of foil line in your Air Fryer basket and add the hash browns on the bottom.

2. Place the uncooked sausage on top. Spread the peppers and onions on top.

3. Place into your Air Fryer and cook at 355°F for about 10 minutes.

4. Carefully open your Air Fryer and mix up the casserole a bit if desired.

5. Crack each egg in a bowl and pour the eggs on top of the casserole.

6. Place into your Air Fryer and cook on 355°F for additional 10 minutes.

7. Serve with salt and pepper to taste.

Breakfast Sandwich

Preparation time: 10 minutes

Cook time: 10 minutes

Total time: 20 minutes

Servings: 4

Ingredients:

- Whole30 Approved Breakfast Patties
- 1 sweet potato, cut into buns
- 4 eggs scrambled
- 1 avocado
- Hot sauce, optional

Cooking Instructions:

1. Preheat the Air Fryer 360°F.

2. Add the cut sweet potato in the Air Fryer.

3. Bake for about 10 minutes. Cook the eggs by heating up the patties on the stove top.

4. Cut up the avocado and form your sandwich.

5. Serve and enjoy!

Baked Apple

Preparation time: 10 minutes

Cook time: 20 minutes

Total time: 30 minutes

Servings: 2

Ingredients:

- 1 medium apple or pear, cut in half and spoon out some flesh
- 2 tablespoons of chopped walnuts
- 2 tablespoons of raisins
- 1 ½ teaspoon of light margarine, melted
- ¼ teaspoon of cinnamon
- ¼ teaspoon of nutmeg
- ¼ cup of water

Cooking Instructions:

1. Preheat your Air Fryer to 350°F.

2. Add the cut apple or pear in frying pan.

3. In a medium bowl, combine together the margarine, cinnamon, nutmeg, walnuts and raisins.

4. Ladle the mixture into the centers of the apple/pear halves. Add the water into the pan. Bake for 20 minutes.

5. Serve and enjoy!

Breakfast Pockets

Ingredients:

- 1 box of puff pastry sheets
- 5 eggs
- ½ cup of sausage crumbles, cooked
- ½ cup of bacon, cooked
- ½ cup of cheddar cheese, shredded

Cooking Instructions:

1. Add meat to the eggs if desired, and cook the eggs as regular scrambled eggs.
2. Spread the puff pastry sheets on a chopping board and cut out rectangles with a sharp knife.
3. Ladle the egg, meat, and cheese combos onto half of the pastry rectangles.
4. Add the pastry rectangle on top of the mixture and fold the edges to seal with a fork.
5. Add the breakfast pockets in your Air Fryer and cook for 8-10 minutes at 370°F.
6. Check every 2 to 3 minutes and cook until your preferred doneness is achieved.
7. Serve and enjoy!

French Toast Sticks

Preparation time: 10 minutes

Cook time: 10 minutes

Total time: 20 minutes

Servings: 2

Ingredients:

- 4 slices slightly stale thick bread, like Texas toast
- 2 eggs, beaten
- ¼ cup of milk
- 1 tsp. of vanilla extract
- 1 tsp. of cinnamon
- 1 pinch ground nutmeg, optional

Cooking Instructions:

1. Cut each slice of bread into thirds to make sticks.

2. Cut a piece of parchment paper and place into the bottom of your Air Fryer basket.

3. Preheat your Air Fryer to 360°F (180°C). In medium bowl, stir together the eggs, milk, vanilla extract, cinnamon, and nutmeg to combine.

4. Add each piece of bread into egg mixture and ensure that the piece of bread is submerge in the egg mixture.

5. Shake each bread stick to drain any excess liquid and add the bread stick to form a single layer in your Air Fryer basket.

6. Cook the bread stick in batches, if desired to prevent overcrowding the Air Fryer.

7. Cook for about 5 minutes, turn the bread pieces, and cook for another 5 minutes.

8. Serve and enjoy!

Breakfast Toad-in-the-Hole Tarts

Preparation time: 5 minutes

Cook time: 25 minutes

Total time: 30 minutes

Servings: 4

Ingredients:

- 1 sheet frozen puff pastry, thawed
- 4 tbsp. of shredded Cheddar cheese
- 4 tbsp. of diced cooked ham
- 4 eggs
- Chopped fresh chives (optional)

Cooking Instructions:

1. Preheat your Air Fryer to 400°F (200°C). Spread the pastry sheet on a flat surface and cut into 4 squares.

2. Add 2 pastry squares in your Air Fryer basket and cook for about 8 minutes. Remove the pastry squares from the Air Fryer basket.

3. Press each square with a fork to form an indentation. Add 1 tbsp. of Cheddar cheese and 1 tbsp. of ham in each hole. Pour 1 egg on top of each.

4. Place back into the Air Fryer basket and cook for about 6 minutes, or until your desired doneness is achieved.

5. Remove tarts from Air Fryer basket and allow to cool for about 5 minutes. Repeat the procedure with the rest of the pastry squares, cheese, ham, and eggs. Garnish tarts with chives.

6. Serve and enjoy!

Cranberry Pecan Muffins

Preparation time: 10 minutes

Cook time: 15 minutes

Total time: 25-35 minutes

Yield: 6-8 muffins

Ingredients:

- ¼ cup of cashew milk (or dairy and non-dairy milk)
- 2 large eggs
- ½ teaspoon of vanilla extract
- 1 ½ cups of Almond Flour
- ¼ cup of Monk fruit (or use your favorite sweetener)
- 1 teaspoon of baking powder
- ¼ teaspoon of cinnamon
- 1/8 teaspoon of salt
- ½ cup of fresh cranberries
- ¼ cup of chopped pecans

Cooking Instructions:

1. Add the milk, eggs and vanilla extract to your blender jar and blend everything for about 20-30 seconds.

2. Add in the almond flour, sugar, baking powder, cinnamon and salt. Blend the ingredients for additional 30-45 seconds or until well blended.

3. Take out the blender jar from the base and add the ½ of the fresh cranberries and the pecans.

4. Pour the mixture into silicone muffin cups and top each of the muffins with the rest of the fresh cranberries.

5. Add the muffin cups into your Air Fryer basket and bake on 325°F for about 12 to 15 minutes. Check for doneness by inserting a toothpick to come out clean.

6. Remove from Air Fryer and place on a cooling rack to cool for a couple of minutes. Drizzle with a maple glaze or melted white chocolate if desired.

7. Serve and enjoy!

Frozen Mozzarella Sticks

Preparation time: 10 minutes

Cook time: 6 minutes

Total time: 16 minutes

Servings: 4

Ingredients:

- Pack Frozen Mozzarella Sticks

Cooking Instructions:

1. Add the frozen mozzarella sticks into basket of your Air Fryer.
2. Cook on 180°C/360°F for about 6 minutes.
3. Serve hot with your desired sauce.

Frozen French Fries

Cook time: 5 minutes

Total time: 5 minutes

Servings: 4

Ingredients:

- Pack McCain's Quick Cook Crispy French Fries
- Pinch of Sea Salt

Cooking Instructions:

1. Preheat your Air Fryer at 180°C/360°F.

2. Add the frozen fries into the Air Fryer basket and cook for about 5 minutes.

3. Serve with sea salt and your desired sauce.

Spicy Sweet Potato Wedges

Preparation time: 5 minutes

Cook time: 20 minutes

Total time: 25 minutes

Servings: 2

Ingredients:

- 2 large sweet potatoes, peeled and chop into shape of wedges
- 1 tablespoon of Mexican seasoning
- 1 teaspoon of cumin
- 1 teaspoon of custard powder
- 1 teaspoon of chili powder
- 1 tablespoon of olive oil
- Pinch of salt
- Pinch of pepper

Cooking Instructions:

1. Preheat the Air Fryer for 5 minutes at 180°C.

2. In a medium bowl, add all the seasonings and give everything a good mix.

3. Add the potato wedges, and add the seasonings. Toss everything until they are well covered.

4. Add the potato wedges into the Air Fryer basket, add in olive oil and cook for 20 minutes.

5. Shake the basket every 5 minutes until they are cooked through.

6. Sprinkle with a little extra chili powder.

7. Serve and enjoy!

Spam Fritters

Preparation time: 5 minutes

Cook time: 8 minutes

Total time: 13 minutes

Servings: 4

Ingredients:

- 400 g Spam, chopped into sticks
- 200 g of gluten free oats
- 100 g of plain flour
- 1 egg, lightly beaten
- 28 g of cheddar cheese
- Pinch of salt
- Pinch of pepper

Cooking Instructions:

1. Add the gluten free oats into the blender and blend.

2. Add the beaten egg in one bowl. Add the plain flour in a separate bowl and gluten free oats in a third.

3. Add the salt and pepper to the flour and give everything a good stir. Add the grated cheddar cheese to your oats and give everything a good stir.

4. Roll in the chopped spam in the flour, roll in the egg and fully coat in the oats.

5. Cook in batches for about 8 minutes at 180°C/360°F.

6. Serve warm and enjoy!

Peanut Butter and Jelly Air Fried Doughnuts

Preparation time: 15 minutes

Cook time: 11 minutes

Total time: 26 minutes

Yield: 6 doughnuts

Ingredients:

Doughnuts Ingredients:

- 1 ¼ cups of all-purpose flour
- 1/3 cup of sugar
- ½ tsp. of baking powder
- ½ tsp. of baking soda
- ¾ tsp. of salt
- 1 egg
- ½ cup of buttermilk
- 1 tsp. of vanilla
- 2 tbsp. of unsalted butter, melted and cooled
- 1 tbsp. of melted butter for brushing the tops

Filling Ingredients:

- ½ cup of Blueberry or strawberry jelly (not preserves)

Glaze Ingredients:

- ½ cup of powdered sugar
- 2 tbsp. of milk
- 2 tbsp. of peanut butter
- Pinch of sea salt

Cooking Instructions:

1. Whisk together the flour, sugar, baking powder, baking soda and salt in a medium bowl.

2. Beat together the egg, melted butter, buttermilk and vanilla in a separate bowl. Make a hole in the center of the dry ingredients and pour in the wet ingredients.

3. Combine the mixture with a fork and stir with a large spoon to incorporate the flour. Flip the dough out onto a well-floured surface.

4. Slightly work the dough to come together and then, pat it out to a 3/4" thickness. Cut out the dough rounds with a 3 1/2" cutter, and brush with the melted butter.

5. Cut out 2" pieces of parchment paper, place each dough round on the paper, and place into the Air Fryer. Cook for about 11 minutes at 350°F.

6. Fill each doughnut with jelly using a pastry bag. Whisk together the glaze ingredients and drizzle over each doughnut.

7. Serve and enjoy!

Flourless Crunchy Onion Rings

Preparation time: 5 minutes

Cook time: 8 minutes

Total time: 13 minutes

Servings: 1

Ingredients:

- 1 cup of gluten free oats
- 1 onion, sliced
- 1 egg, beaten
- Salt to taste
- Pepper to taste

Cooking Instructions:

1. Preheat the Air Fryer to 180°C and add the beaten egg in a medium bowl.

2. Blend the gluten free oats in a food processor into fine breadcrumbs. Add them into a medium bowl.

3. Slice your onion into whole slices and push out the rings onto your chopping board.

4. Dip in the oats, in the egg and then, back into the oats. Add into the Air Fryer basket and cook at 180°C for 8 minutes.

5. Serve and enjoy!

Breakfast Potatoes

Preparation time: 5 minutes

Cook time: 15 minutes

Total time: 20 minutes

Servings: 4

Ingredients:

- 3 large white potatoes, peeled and cubed
- 1 white onion, diced
- 6 slices of back bacon, diced
- 2.5 ml of olive oil
- 2 teaspoons of parsley
- Salt & Pepper

Cooking Instructions:

1. Add the bacon, onion and seasoning into the mixing bowl and give everything a good mix.

2. Add the olive oil and give everything a good mix. Add the bowl containing the ingredients in your Air Fryer basket.

3. Cook at 180°C/360°F for 15 minutes. Shake the potatoes when they are half way cooked to avoid sticking.

4. Serve warm and enjoy!

Breaded Dill Pickle Chips

Preparation time: 4 minutes

Cook time: 8 minutes

Total time: 10 minutes

Servings: 2

Ingredients:

- 1 Jar dill pickles, chopped
- 200 g of gluten free oats
- 1 teaspoon of basil
- Salt & Pepper

Cooking Instructions:

1. Chop the dill pickles into thirds and leave the pickle juice from them.

2. Blend the gluten free oats, salt, pepper and basil in your blender until it resembles breadcrumbs. Pour the mixture into a large bowl.

3. Add the dill pickles into the dry ingredients and stir to coat. Add the dill pickles into your Air Fryer.

4. Cook at 200°C/400°F for 4 minutes on each side.

5. Serve warm and enjoy!

Blueberry Lemon Muffin

Preparation time: 5 minutes

Cook time: 10 minutes

Total time: 25 minutes

Yield: 1

Ingredients:

- 2 ½ cups of self-rising flour
- ½ cup of Monk Fruit
- ½ cup of cream
- ¼ cup of avocado oil
- 2 eggs
- 1 cup of blueberries
- Zest from 1 lemon
- Juice from 1 lemon
- 1 teaspoon of vanilla
- Brown sugar for topping

Cooking Instructions:

1. Mix together the self-rising flour and sugar in a medium bowl and set aside.

2. In a separate bowl, combine together the cream, oil, lemon juice, eggs and vanilla.

3. Add the flour mixture to the liquid mixture and give everything a good stir to blend.

4. Stir in the blueberries and ladle the batter into silicone cupcake holders. Sprinkle with ½ teaspoon of brown sugar on top of each muffin.

5. Place in your Air Fryer and bake at 320°F for 10 minutes. Check the muffins at 6 minutes to avoid cooking very fast.

6. Check for doneness by inserting a toothpick into the center of the muffin to come out clean.

7. The muffins should be browned. Remove and allow to cool for a couple of minutes.

8. Serve and enjoy!

Pitta Pizza

Preparation time: 3 minutes

Cook time: 3 minutes

Total time: 6 minutes

Servings: 4

Ingredients:

- 4 Whole meal Pittas
- 4 slices of gouda cheese
- 200 g of tinned tomatoes
- 1 teaspoon of tomato puree
- 3 garlic cloves, peeled and quartered
- Pinch of oregano
- Salt & pepper
- Fresh basil

Cooking Instructions:

1. Add the fresh basil, garlic, tomato puree and tinned tomatoes in the blender and blend until smooth.

2. Season with salt and pepper. Add a layer of tomato sauce over the pittas with a pastry brush.

3. Add 1 slice of cheese and sprinkle with oregano. Place in your Air Fryer grill pan.

4. Cook at 160°C/320°F for 3 minutes.

5. Serve and enjoy!

Rosemary Roast Potatoes

Preparation time: 2 minutes

Cook time: 10 minutes

Total time: 12 minutes

Servings: 4

Ingredients:

- 2 large potatoes, peel and cut into roast potato shapes
- 1 teaspoon of rosemary
- 1 tablespoon of olive oil
- Salt & Pepper

Cooking Instructions:

1. Add the potatoes in your Air Fryer basket.

2. Cook at 180°C for 10 minutes with a tablespoon of olive oil.

3. Check for doneness and add them in a mixing bowl.

4. Sprinkle with the rosemary and the salt and pepper. Give everything a good mix.

5. Serve and enjoy!

Mini Cheese Scones

Preparation time: 5 minutes

Cook time: 20 minutes

Total time: 25 minutes

Servings: 10

Ingredients:

- 175 g of self-rising flour
- 25 g of butter
- 1 egg
- 1 tablespoon of whole milk
- 75 g of cheddar cheese
- 1 teaspoon of mustard
- 1 teaspoon of chives
- Salt & Pepper

Cooking Instructions:

1. Preheat the Air Fryer at 180°C. In a medium bowl, mix together the flour and butter until it resembles fine breadcrumbs.

2. Add the seasoning along with 50g of the cheddar cheese and give everything good mix. Add the milk and egg and give everything good mix.

3. Use your hands to make the mixture resembles a soft dough. Add a little milk if the mixture is not soft.

4. Ensure that it is 1.5cm thick and divide them into 10 equal pieces. Add a little of the leftover cheese into the middle of them and form them into balls.

5. Add the mini scones into the Air Fryer. Cook at 180°C for 20 minutes. Slice in half and add a little bit of butter in the center of each.

6. Serve and enjoy!

Cheesy Homemade Garlic Bread

Preparation time: 5 minutes

Cook time: 20 minutes

Total time: 25 minutes

Servings: 4

Ingredients:

- 10 inch of Homemade Pizza Dough
- 125 g of butter
- 1 teaspoon of garlic puree
- 125 g of cream cheese
- 1 teaspoon of parsley
- Salt & Pepper

Cooking Instructions:

1. Roll out the pizza dough to be ready for topping.
2. Place a layer of soft cheese on your base.
3. In a pan on a medium heat, add the butter to melt.
4. Mix with the garlic puree, parsley, salt and pepper.
5. Place the garlic butter mixture on top of the cream cheese and place in the Air Fryer.
6. Cook at 180°C for 20 minutes.
7. Serve and enjoy!

AIR FRYER MAIN MEALS

Sweet Potato Fries

Preparation time: 5 minutes

Cook time: 15 minutes

Total time: 20 minutes

Servings: 2

Ingredients:

- 300 g of sweet potatoes, peeled and chopped into chunky chips
- 3 tablespoons of olive oil
- 1 teaspoon of mustard powder
- Salt & Pepper

Cooking Instructions:

1. Add the chopped potatoes in the Air Fryer along with 2 tbsp. of olive oil.
2. Shake the potatoes to be well covered with the oil. Cook at 180°C for 15 minutes.
3. Shake the potatoes when they are half way cooked to avoid sticking to the bottom.
4. Add the potatoes in a medium bowl when cooked. Add the remaining 1 tbsp. of olive oil along with the seasoning.
5. Give everything a good mix with your hands or by shaking the dish.
6. Serve and enjoy!

Roasted Brussels Sprouts

Preparation time: 5 minutes

Cook time: 18 minutes

Total time: 23 minutes

Serves: 2

Ingredients:

- 1 lb. of Brussels sprouts
- 1 ½ tbsp. of olive oil
- ½ tsp. of salt
- ½ tsp. of black pepper

Cooking Instructions:

1. Preheat your Air Fryer at 390°F. Wash the Brussels sprouts in clean water and pat dry with a towel.

2. Discard the loose leaves and cut the sprouts in half if they are larger. Add the Brussels sprouts into a medium bowl.

3. Drizzle with the olive oil over the vegetables and give everything a good stir to coat the Brussel sprouts.

4. Season with salt and pepper. Add the Brussels sprouts in the Air Fryer basket.

5. Cook for 15 to 18 minutes or until the Brussels sprouts start to turn brown and soften.

6. Serve and enjoy!

Parmesan Truffle Oil Fries

Preparation time: 10 minutes

Cook time: 40 minutes

Total time: 50 minutes

Servings: 6

Ingredients:

- 3 large russet potatoes, peeled and cut lengthwise
- 2 tablespoons of white truffle oil
- 2 tablespoons of parmesan shredded
- 1 teaspoon of paprika
- Salt and pepper to taste
- 1 tablespoon of parsley, chopped

Cooking Instructions:

1. Add the sliced potatoes in a medium bowl along with cold water. Let the potatoes to soak for about 30 minutes.

2. Layer the fries onto a flat surface and pat dry with a paper towels. Add the 1 tablespoon of white truffle oil and seasonings and toss everything to coat.

3. Add half of the fries to the Air Fryer basket. Cook at 380°F for 15 to 20 minutes. Shake the basket at the 10-minute mark.

4. Remove them from the basket and add the remaining truffle oil and parmesan to the fries. Top with shredded parsley.

5. Serve and enjoy!

Kale Chips

Ingredients:

- 1 bunch of kale with steam removed, and chopped into bite pieces
- 2-3 tbsp. of olive oil
- 2 tbsp. of nutritional yeast optional
- ½ tsp. of salt

Cooking Instructions:

1. Add the chopped kale pieces in to a bowl or zip lock bag.
2. Toss everything to coat with the oil. Add the seasonings and place in the Air Fryer.
3. Cook at 275°C for 15 to 17 minutes, stirring at half mark interval.
4. Serve and enjoy!

Rich Fruit Scones

Preparation time: 5 minutes

Cook time: 8 minutes

Total time: 13 minutes

Servings: 4

Ingredients:

- 225 g of Self Raising Flour
- 50 g of butter
- 50 g of sultanas
- 25 g of caster sugar
- 1 egg
- Milk

Cooking Instructions:

1. In a medium bowl, toss together the flour and butter and rub the fat into the flour.

2. Add the sultanas, caster sugar and crack the egg into the mixture.

3. Give the mixture a good mix with a fork to combine. Add the milk a little at a time to make a smooth scone dough.

4. Use your hands to form the dough into scone shapes. Place in your Air Fryer grill pan.

5. Cook for about 8 minutes at 180°C/360°F.

6. Serve warm and enjoy!

Gyro Meatballs

Preparation time: 15 minutes

Cook time: 11 minutes

Total time: 26 minutes

Serves: 35-40

Ingredients:

- 1 pound of ground lamb
- 1 pound of ground beef (We used 93/7)
- 1 egg, whisked
- 1 tbsp. of rosemary
- 1 tbsp. of oregano
- 1 tbsp. of dried dill
- Juice of 1 lemon
- 2 garlic cloves, minced
- Salt and pepper to taste
- Nonstick cooking spray

Cooking Instructions:

1. Add all the meatball ingredients in your food processor. Make the mixture into about 1 inch balls.

2. Spray the basket of your Air Fryer with nonstick cooking spray. Add the meatballs in Air Fryer.

3. Cook for 7 minutes at 350°F. Remove the basket out, and shake meatballs.

4. Place the basket back into the Air Fryer and cook for additional 4 minutes.

5. Allow to cool for a couple of minutes before serving.

6. Serve and enjoy!

Spanish Spicy Potatoes

Preparation time: 10 minutes

Cook time: 23 minutes

Total time: 33 minutes

Servings: 4

Ingredients:

- 3 large potatoes, peeled and chopped into chips
- 1 medium onion, peeled and diced
- 100 ml of homemade tomato sauce
- 1 tomato, thinly diced
- 1 tablespoon of red wine vinegar
- 2 tablespoons of olive oil
- 1 teaspoon of paprika
- 1 teaspoon of chili powder
- 2 teaspoons of coriander
- 2 teaspoons of thyme
- 1 teaspoon of mixed spice
- 1 teaspoon of oregano
- 1 teaspoon of rosemary
- Salt & Pepper

Cooking Instructions:

1. Add the chips along with the olive oil in the Air Fryer.

2. Cook at 180°C for 15 minutes. Meanwhile, prepare the sauce while they are cooking.

3. In a medium bowl, mix together the remaining ingredients. Remove the potatoes when the Air Fryer is dine cooking.

4. Add the tomato sauce in Air Fryer baking dish and cook for 8 minutes at 180°C.

5. Pour the sauce over the potatoes when they are dine cooking.

6. Serve and enjoy!

Sausage Rolls

Preparation time: 5 minutes

Cook time: 10 minutes

Total time: 15 minutes

Servings: 4

Ingredients:

- Pasty Maker
- 2.5 Weight Watchers Wraps
- 200 g of minced pork
- 1 egg, beaten
- 2 teaspoon of thyme
- Salt & Pepper

Cooking Instructions:

1. In a medium bowl, mix together the minced pork and the seasonings.

2. Use your hands to give everything a good mix. Form the mixture into the shape of a sausage meat roll.

3. Refrigerate for at least 10 minutes to stiffen up. Add the Weight Watchers Wrap onto a clean worktop. Brush it with beaten egg.

4. Place the filling in the center and roll it up to form a Swiss roll. Cover it with egg and place in the Air Fryer.

5. Cook at 200°C/400°F for 5 minutes.

6. Serve warm and enjoy!

Cheese & Onion Pasties

Preparation time: 5 minutes

Cook time: 12 minutes

Total time: 17 minutes

Servings: 8

Ingredients:

- Pasty Maker
- 4 Weight Watchers Wraps
- 2 large potatoes, peeled and thinly diced
- 1 medium white onion, diced
- 1 egg, beaten
- 80 g of diet cheddar cheese
- 60 g of Cheshire cheese
- 1 tablespoon of chives
- Salt & Pepper

Cooking Instructions:

1. Add the diced potatoes and onion into the bottom of your Instant Pot. Pour 1 cup of water (250ml).

2. Close and lock the lid in place and ensure that the valve is in sealing position. Select Manual, High Pressure for 8 minutes.

3. Grate the cheese and slice your wraps in half. When the timer beeps, do a natural pressure release for about 10 minutes.

4. Carefully open the lid and drain the potatoes and onion. Add them back into the bottom of your Instant Pot.

5. Add the seasoning and the grated cheese and give everything a good mix. Add ½ a wrap at a time into the pasty press and brush with egg.

6. Add the pasty filling to one side and ensure that they don't over fill it. Press it down to form a pasty shape. Brush the outside with egg.

7. Place them in your Air Fryer. Cook at 200°C/400°F for 2 minutes on each side.

8. Serve warm and enjoy!

Chewy Granola Bars

Preparation time: 3 minutes

Cook time: 15 minutes

Total time: 18 minutes

Servings: 6

Ingredients:

- 250 g of gluten free oats
- 60 g of melted butter
- 30 g of brown sugar
- 3 tablespoons of honey
- 1 medium apple, peeled & cooked
- 1 tablespoon of olive oil
- 1 teaspoon of vanilla essence
- 1 teaspoon of cinnamon
- Handful raisins

Cooking Instructions:

1. Add the gluten free oats in a blender and blend until smooth. Add the remaining dry ingredients to the blender.

2. Add all the wet ingredients to your Air Fryer basket and give everything a good stir with wooden spoon.

3. Pour out the dry ingredients from the blender and into the baking pan. Give everything a good mix with a fork.

4. Add the raisins and press down the mixture into the baking pan. Cook at 160°C/320°F for 10 minutes.

5. Cook for additional 5 minutes at 180°C/360°F. Refrigerate for about 5 minutes to stiffen up. Chop into chewy granola bars and serve.

6. Serve and enjoy!

Roasted Swede

Preparation time: 2 minutes

Cook time: 18 minutes

Total time: 20 minutes

Servings: 4

Ingredients:

- 1 large swede, peeled and diced
- 1 teaspoon of garlic puree
- 1 tablespoon of parsley
- Salt & Pepper

Cooking Instructions:

1. Add the swede into your Instant Pot steamer basket.
2. Add the steamer basket into the bottom of your Instant Pot and pour 1 cup of warm water.
3. Close and lock the lid in place and ensure that the valve is in sealing position. Select Manual, High Pressure for 4 minutes.
4. When the timer beeps, do a quick pressure release.
5. Carefully open the lid and drain the swede. Mix in the garlic puree and the seasoning.
6. Place in the Air Fryer basket. Cook at 180°C/360°F for 14 minutes.
7. Serve and enjoy!

Garlic Parsley Potatoes

Preparation time: 5 minutes

Cook time: 35 minutes

Total time: 40 minutes

Servings: 3

Ingredients:

- 3 Idaho or Russet Baking Potatoes
- 1-2 tbsp. of olive oil
- 1 tbsp. of salt
- 1 tbsp. of garlic
- 1 tsp. of parsley

Cooking Instructions:

1. Wash the potatoes and make air holes with a fork in the potatoes.
2. Sprinkle the potatoes with olive oil and seasonings.
3. Rub the seasoning on the potatoes to coat.
4. Add the potatoes in the Air Fryer basket.
5. Cook at 392°F for about 35 to 40 minutes or until tender. Top with fresh parsley and sour cream if desired.
6. Serve and enjoy!

Seasoned Asparagus

Preparation time: 2 minutes

Cook time: 10 minutes

Total time: 12 minutes

Servings: 4

Ingredients:

- 1 bunch of asparagus, trim about 2 inches of the stems
- Olive oil cooking spray
- Dash of garlic salt

Cooking Instructions:

1. Place the trimmed asparagus to the Air Fryer basket.

2. Sprinkle with olive oil spray and a dash of garlic salt and toss to coat.

3. Cook for 5 minutes at 390°F. Check the asparagus and turn it to cook for another 5 minutes.

4. Serve and enjoy!

Rock Buns

Preparation time: 5 minutes

Cook time: 10 minutes

Total time: 15 minutes

Servings: 8

Ingredients:

- Lemon zester
- 225 g of self-rising flour
- 100 g of butter
- 50 g of caster sugar
- 1 medium egg
- 75 g of mixed raisins
- 1 medium lemon
- 1 medium orange
- 1 tablespoon of honey
- Milk

Cooking Instructions:

1. In a medium bowl, add the flour, sugar and butter and rub the fat into the flour.

2. Add the raisins and honey. Place the lemon and orange rind in a grater. Chop them in half and drain the juice into the bowl too.

3. Give everything a good mix with a fork. Crack the egg in and give everything a good mix.

4. Add the milk a little bit at a time to form a soft dough. Form the dough shapes into small scone shapes.

5. Add in your Air Fryer grill pan. Cook for 10 minutes at 180°C/360°F.

6. Serve warm and enjoy!

AIR FRYER POULTRY RECIPES

Chicken Schnitzel

Preparation time: 6 minutes

Cook time: 12 minutes

Total time: 18 minutes

Servings: 4

Ingredients:

- 2 chicken breast
- 12 tablespoons of gluten free oats
- 2 small eggs
- 2 teaspoons of mustard powder
- Salt & pepper
- Fresh parsley
- Garlic potatoes, optional
- Lemon wedges, optional

Cooking Instructions:

1. Add the chicken breasts onto a clean chopping board and flatten out the chicken to make 4 flat pieces of chicken breast.

2. Season with salt and pepper on each side. Beat 2 eggs with a fork and add them in a medium bowl.

3. Add the gluten free oats, salt and pepper, mustard and the fresh parsley in your blender and blend until it resembles breadcrumbs.

4. Add the blended ingredients into another dish. Roll the chicken in the oats, then the egg and then back in the oats.

5. Add the chicken in your Air Fryer grill pan. Cook for 12 minutes at 180°C (360°F). Shake them when they are cooked half way with some tongs.

6. Serve with some warm potatoes and enjoy!

Chicken Tikka

Preparation time: 3 minutes

Cook time: 10 minutes

Total time: 13 minutes

Servings: 4

Ingredients:

- 2 large chicken breasts

Chicken Tikka Marinade:

- 1 teaspoon of grated ginger
- 2 teaspoons of garlic puree
- ½ medium diced onion
- Pinch of chili
- 2 teaspoons of Garam masala
- 2 teaspoons of paprika
- 2 teaspoons of turmeric
- 2 teaspoons of cumin
- Juice & rind of 1 lemon
- 300 ml of Greek yoghurt

Cooking Instructions:

1. In a medium bowl, add together the chicken tikka marinade ingredients and give everything a good mix until an even marinade is formed.

2. Place the chicken breasts and let to marinade overnight. Remove the chicken from the marinade the next day.

3. Place the chicken on a chopping board and chop them into the shapes of chicken tikka bite.

4. Place in your Air Fryer grill pan. Cook for 10 minutes at 180°C/360°F.

5. Serve warm and enjoy!

Mini Turkey Pies

Preparation time: 2 minutes

Cook time: 10 minutes

Total time: 12 minutes

Servings: 8

Ingredients:

- 8 slices of filo pastry
- 50 g of shredded turkey
- 1 medium egg, beaten
- 50 ml of coconut milk
- 50 ml of whole milk
- 200 ml homemade tomato sauce
- 20 ml of turkey stock
- 1 teaspoon of oregano
- 1 tablespoon of coriander
- Salt & Pepper

Cooking Instructions:

1. In a medium bowl, add the wet ingredients except for the egg and give everything a good mix.

2. Add the turkey and seasoning and give everything a good mix again. Set the mixture aside.

3. Line the small pie cases with a little flour to prevent them from sticking to the bottom and then line with the filo pastry.

4. Line one sheet of filo for each pie and have it centered to fold over the spare pastry for the top of the pie.

5. Pour the mixture to each mini pie pot and ensure that they are ¾ full. Fill the top with the rest of the pastry.

6. Brush the egg along the top and place in the Air Fryer. Cook at 180°C for 10 minutes.

7. Serve and enjoy!

KFC Chicken Strips

Preparation time: 10 minutes

Cook time: 12 minutes

Total time: 22 minutes

Servings: 8

Ingredients:

- 1 chicken breast, chopped into strips
- 15 ml of desiccated coconut
- 15 ml of plain oats
- 5 ml of KFC spice blend
- 75 ml of bread crumbs
- 50 g of plain flour
- 1 medium e gg, beaten
- Salt & Pepper

Cooking Instructions:

1. In a medium bowl, add together the coconut, oats, KFC spice blend, bread crumbs and salt and pepper.

2. In a separate bowl, beat the egg and in another your plain flour.

3. Add the strips in the plain flour, then in the egg and in the spicy layer.

4. Add them in your Air Fryer. Cook for 8 minutes at 180°C.

5. Cook for additional 4 minutes at 160°C to cook at the center.

6. Serve and enjoy!

Chicken Wrapped In Bacon

Preparation time: 3 minutes

Cook time: 15 minutes

Total time: 18 minutes

Servings: 6

Ingredients:

- 6 back bacon
- 1 chicken breast
- 1 tablespoon of garlic soft cheese

Cooking Instructions:

1. Chop the chicken breast into six smaller sized pieces.

2. Take the bacon rashers and spread them with a small layer of soft cheese.

3. Add the chicken on top of the cheese and roll them up. Place a cocktail stick to secure them.

4. Add them in your Air Fryer. Cook at 180°C for 15 minutes.

5. Serve and enjoy!

Lemon Pepper Chicken

Preparation time: 3 minutes

Cook time: 15 minutes

Total time: 18 minutes

Servings: 1

Ingredients:

- 1 chicken breast
- 2 lemons rind and juice
- 1 tablespoon of chicken seasoning
- 1 teaspoon of garlic puree
- Handful black peppercorns
- Salt & pepper

Cooking Instructions:

1. Preheat your Air Fryer to 180°C. Spread a sheet of silver foil on the work top and add all the seasonings and the lemon rind.

2. Place the chicken breasts onto a chopping board and trim off any fatty bits. Season the chicken breasts with salt and pepper on both sides.

3. Rub the chicken seasoning on each side and add them on the sheet of silver foil. Seal the content very tight to get the flavor into it.

4. Take a rolling pin to give it a slap to flatten it out to release more flavor. Place them in your Air Fryer.

5. Cook at 180°C for 15 minutes. Check for doneness and ensure that the middle is cook through.

6. Serve and enjoy!

Buffalo Chicken Legs

Servings: 2

Ingredients:

- 2 pounds of chicken drumsticks (skin removed)
- 2 tbsp. of ghee (melted)
- ¼ cup of Frank's Red Hot Original Sauce

Cooking Instructions:

1. Preheat your Air Fryer at 400°F for 2-13 minutes. Take a nonstick oil to spray your Air Fryer basket.

2. Add the chicken drumsticks in the Air Fryer basket. Cook for 15 minutes at 400°F. Turn the drumsticks and cook at 400°F for additional 5 minutes.

3. In a medium bowl, mix together the melted ghee and hot sauce. Remove the drumsticks to bowl and toss in sauce.

4. Add the drumsticks back into the Air Fryer basket and ladle the rest of the sauce over the top of the drumsticks.

5. Cook at 165°F for additional 5 minutes or until internal chicken temperature is 165°F.

6. Serve with Whole30 Ranch Dip, celery and carrots and enjoy!

Frozen Chicken Wings

Cook time: 12 minutes

Total time: 12 minutes

Servings: 4

Ingredients:

- Pack Chicken Wings

Cooking Instructions:

1. Preheat the Air Fryer to 180°C/360°F for 2-3 minutes.
2. Add the frozen chicken wings into the Air Fryer basket.
3. Cook for 12 minutes at 180°C/360°F.
4. Serve warm with your desired sauce.

Chicken Fried Rice

Ingredients:

- 3 cups of cooked white rice cold
- 1 cup of cooked chicken, diced
- 1 cup of frozen peas and carrots
- 6 tablespoons of soy sauce
- 1 tablespoon of vegetable oil
- ½ cup of onion, diced

Cooking Instructions:

1. In a medium bowl, add the cold cooked white rice and vegetable oil.

2. Add the soy sauce and give everything a good mix. Add the frozen peas & carrots, the diced onion and the diced chicken.

3. Give everything a good mix and add the rice mixture into the nonstick pan. Place the pan in the Air Fryer.

4. Cook at 360°F for 20 minutes. Remove the pan from the Air Fryer and check for doneness.

5. Serve with your desired meat and enjoy!

Honey Garlic Chicken Wings

Preparation time: 5 minutes

Cook time: 20 minutes

Total time: 25 minutes

Servings: 8-10 pieces

Ingredients:

- 1 ½ pounds of chicken wings
- 2 tablespoons of soy sauce
- ¼ cup of potato starch
- 3 cloves garlic
- 1 tablespoon of butter
- 3 tablespoons of honey
- ½ teaspoon of salt
- 1 teaspoon of red pepper flakes

Cooking Instructions:

1. Toss the chicken wings together with soy sauce and reserve aside. Preheat your Air Fryer for a couple of minutes.

2. Add the potato starch in a large zip top plastic bag and add the chicken wings. Shake the content very well to coat the chicken wings with potato starch.

3. Spray the Air Fryer basket with oil and layer the wings in basket, shaking off any excess potato starch.

4. Cook in batches if desired. Cook for 15 minutes at 370°F. Shake the Air Fryer basket and cook at 400°F for additional 5 minutes.

5. Place the garlic and butter in a microwave and microwave for 30 seconds, or until melted.

6. Add the honey and season with a pinch of salt and red pepper flakes. Add the wings in sauce.

7. Serve and enjoy!

Crispy Chicken Nuggets

Preparation time: 10 minutes

Cook time: 10 minutes

Total time: 20 minutes

Servings: 15

Ingredients:

- 1 chicken breast
- 1 large egg, beaten
- 1 cup of gluten free oats
- 1 tablespoon of thyme
- 1 tablespoon of parsley
- Salt & Pepper

Cooking Instructions:

1. Preheat the Air Fryer to 180°C. Add the chicken breast into a blender and blend until it looks like minced chicken.

2. Add into a medium bowl to make the chicken nuggets. Place your egg in a separate bowl.

3. Add the oats in your blender or food processor and blend until it looks like breadcrumbs.

4. In the chicken bowl, season with salt, pepper, parsley and thyme and give everything a good mix.

5. Take a chicken nugget sized piece of the chicken mixture and form them you're your desired shapes with your hands.

6. Add it in the blended oats, then in the egg and then back in the oats and set aside.

7. Repeat the same procedure for all the chicken nuggets and add them on a baking sheet in your Air Fryer. Cook for 10 minutes at 180°C.

8. Serve with tomato ketchup and mustard and enjoy!

Buttermilk Chicken

Ingredients:

- 800 g of store-bought chicken thighs (skin on, bone in)

Marinade Ingredients:

- 2 cups of buttermilk
- 2 tsp. of salt
- 2 tsp. of black pepper
- 1 tsp. of cayenne pepper (We used paprika powder)
- Seasoned Flour
- 2 cups of all-purpose flour
- 1 tbsp. of baking powder
- 1 tbsp. of garlic powder
- 1 tbsp. of paprika powder
- 1 tsp. of salt

Cooking Instructions:

1. Rinse the chicken thighs in water and drain any fat and residue. Pat the chicken thighs dry with paper towels.

2. In a medium bowl, add together the chicken pieces, black pepper, paprika and salt and give everything a good mix to coat.

3. Add the buttermilk over until chicken is coated. Place in the fridge to refrigerate for at least 6 hours or overnight.

4. Preheat your Air Fryer at 180°C. In another bowl, combine together the flour, baking powder, paprika and salt and pepper.

5. Remove the chicken, from the buttermilk and dredge in seasoned flour. Remove any excess flour and place to a bowl.

6. Layer the chicken in a single layer in your Air Fryer basket, skin side up. Cook for 8 minutes at 180°C.

7. Remove the tray, turn chicken pieces over, and cook for additional 10 minutes. Let to drain on paper towels.

8. Serve and enjoy!

Chinese Chicken Wings

Preparation time: 5 minutes

Cook time: 30 minutes

Total time: 35 minutes

Servings: 2

Ingredients:

- 4 chicken wings
- 1 tablespoon of soy sauce
- 1 teaspoon of mixed spice
- 1 tablespoon of Chinese spice
- Salt & Pepper

Cooking Instructions:

1. In a medium bowl, add the seasoning and give everything a good stir to mix and blend.

2. Place the chicken wings and mix the seasoning over the chicken. Rub the seasoning into the chicken wings to coat.

3. Add a sheet of silver foil into the bottom of your Air Fryer and add the chicken on top. Pour over any remaining seasoning.

4. Cook for 15 minutes at 180°C. Turn the chicken over and cook for additional 15 minutes at 200°C.

5. Serve and enjoy!

KFC Popcorn Chicken

Preparation time: 10 minutes

Cook time: 12 minutes

Total time: 22 minutes

Servings: 12

Ingredients:

- 1 chicken breast
- 2 ml of KFC spice blend
- 60 ml of bread crumbs
- 1 medium egg, beaten
- 50 g of plain flour
- Salt & Pepper

Cooking Instructions:

1. Add the chicken in your food processor and blend until it looks like minced chicken.

2. Place the flour in a bowl, and another bowl with the beaten egg and the third bowl with the KFC spice blend, salt and pepper and then your bread crumbs.

3. Make the minced chicken into balls and roll in the flour, the egg and then the spiced bread crumbs.

4. Place in your Air Fryer and cook for 10 to 12 minutes at 180°C or the middle is cooked through.

5. Serve and enjoy!

Turkey Spring Rolls

Preparation time: 33 minutes

Cook time: 5 minutes

Total time: 38 minutes

Servings: 8

Ingredients:

- 2 tortilla wraps
- 30 g of leftover turkey breast, shredded
- 2 large eggs, beaten
- 1 tablespoon of honey
- 1 tablespoon of soy sauce
- 1 teaspoon of Worcester sauce
- 1 teaspoon of coriander
- 1 tablespoon of Chinese five spice
- Salt & Pepper

Cooking Instructions:

1. In a medium bowl, add together the leftover turkey along with all the seasonings. Give everything a good mix with your hands to coat.

2. Roll out your tortilla wraps and brush them with a little water on each side and then again with the egg.

3. Refrigerate for at least 30 minutes to absorb the egg properly. Remove from the fridge after 30 minutes and cut them up into 8 separate spring roll sheets.

4. Fill the turkey filling into each of them and roll them up like a spring roll. Brush them with another layer of egg and place them in your Air Fryer.

5. Cook for 5 minutes at 180°C.

6. Serve and enjoy!

AIR FRYER FISH & SEAFOOD RECIPES

Lemon Garlic Shrimp

Preparation time: 5 minutes

Cook time: 5 minutes

Total time: 10 minutes

Yields: 4

Ingredients:

- 1 lb. of small shrimp, peeled with tails removed
- 1 tbsp. of olive oil
- 4 garlic cloves, minced
- 1 lemon, zested and juiced
- 1 pinch crushed red pepper flakes (optional)
- ¼ cup of parsley, chopped
- ¼ tsp. of sea salt

Cooking Instructions:

1. Preheat the Air Fryer to 400°F.

2. In a medium bowl, combine together the shrimp, olive oil, garlic, salt, lemon zest, and red pepper flakes (if desired).

3. Toss everything to coat. Place the shrimp into the Air Fryer basket.

4. Cook at 400°F for 5-8 minutes, shaking the basket halfway through, or until the shrimp are cooked through.

5. Add the shrimp into a serving plate and add the lemon juice and parsley. Season with more salt to taste.

6. Serve and enjoy!

Fried Catfish

Preparation time: 5 minutes

Cook time: 1 hour

Total time: 1 hour 5 minutes

Servings: 4

Ingredients:

- 4 catfish fillets, rinsed and pat dry
- ¼ cup of seasoned fish fry, We used Louisiana
- 1 tablespoon of olive oil
- 1 tablespoon of chopped parsley, optional

Cooking Instructions:

1. Preheat your Air Fryer to 400°F. Rinse the catfish in clean water and pat dry with a paper towel.

2. Place the fish fry seasoning in a large Ziploc bag and add the catfish to the bag. Seal the bag and shake to coat the filet with the seasoning.

3. Spray each of the fillet with olive oil. Place the fillet in your Air Fryer basket.

4. Cook for 10 minutes. Turn the fish and cook for another 10 minutes.

5. Turn the fish and cook for more 2 to 3 minutes or until desired crispness. Top with parsley.

6. Serve and enjoy!

Air Fryer Salmon

Preparation time: 5 minutes

Cook time: 10 minutes

Total time: 15 minutes

Servings: 2

Ingredients:

- 2 pink salmon fillets
- Cooking spray
- ½ teaspoon of paprika
- Ground cardamom pinch
- Salt to taste
- Black pepper to taste

Cooking Instructions:

1. Preheat your Air Fryer to 350°F/180°C.

2. Use a cooking spray to spray the salmon fillets and sprinkle on the paprika, ground cardamom, salt and pepper.

3. Place the salmon fillets in your Air Fryer basket. Cook for 8 to 12 minutes.

4. Check for your desired doneness. Turn the fillets halfway through cook time.

5. Serve and enjoy!

Crispy Coconut Prawns

Preparation time: 3 minutes

Cook time: 15 minutes

Total time: 18 minutes

Servings: 1

Ingredients:

- 30 king prawns
- 1 small cauliflower
- 2 tablespoons of garlic puree
- 1 large lemon pureed
- 2 tablespoons of coconut oil
- 1 teaspoon of red Thai curry paste
- 2 tablespoons of coriander
- 1 tablespoon of mixed spice
- 1 teaspoon of Chinese 5 spice
- 1 medium lemon
- Salt & Pepper

Cooking Instructions:

1. Wash the king prawns and add them in a medium bowl. Melt the coconut oil in a frying pan and add the prawns.

2. Add the garlic puree into for 2 minutes and add them into the mixing bowl. Add the lemon, red Thai curry paste, salt and pepper and give everything a good mix.

3. Cover the bowl with cling film and refrigerate for at least 1 hour. Meanwhile, make the breadcrumbs while the prawns is cooking.

4. Add the cauliflower in your blender and blend until it looks like breadcrumbs. Add the remaining seasoning with more extra salt and pepper.

5. Pour the mixture into the mixing bowl ready for breading your prawns. Beat the egg in a separate bowl. Remove the prawns and pat dry with paper towel.

6. Place them in the breadcrumbs, then in the egg and then back in the breadcrumbs. Place in your Air Fryer. Cook at 180°C for 10 minutes.

7. Serve with fresh lemon and enjoy!

Shrimp Scampi

Preparation time: 5 minutes

Cook time: 10 minutes

Total time: 15 minutes

Servings: 4

Ingredients:

- 4 tbsp. of butter
- 1 tbsp. of lemon juice
- 1 tbsp. of minced garlic
- 2 tsp. of red pepper flakes
- 1 tbsp. of chopped chives or 1 tsp. of dried chives
- 1 tbsp. of minced basil leaves or 1 tsp. of dried basil
- 2 tbsp. of chicken stock (or white wine)
- 1 pound of defrosted shrimp (21-25 count)

Cooking Instructions:

1. Preheat your Air Fryer to 330°F.

2. Place a 6 x 3 metal pan and add the butter, garlic, and red pepper flakes.

3. Allow it to cook for 2 minutes, stirring, to melt the butter.

4. Add all the ingredients into the pan and place into the Air Fryer, stirring gently.

5. Let the shrimp cook for 5 about minutes, stirring once.

6. Give everything a good mix and remove the 6-inch pan from the Air Fryer.

7. Allow the pan to sit for a couple of minutes to enable the shrimp cook in the residual heat.

8. Give everything a good stir and sprinkle with more fresh basil leaves.

9. Serve and enjoy!

Homemade Cajun Breakfast Sausage

Preparation time: 5 minutes

Cook time: 40 minutes

Total time: 45 minutes

Servings: 12-14

Ingredients:

- 1.5 pounds of ground sausage (chicken sausage or lean pork)
- 1 teaspoon of chili flakes
- Fresh thyme 2 teaspoons of fresh leaves only or ½ teaspoon 1 teaspoon of dried thyme
- 1 teaspoon of onion powder
- ½ teaspoon of each paprika and cayenne
- ¼ teaspoon of sea salt or black pepper
- Chopped sage (optional)
- 2 teaspoons of brown sugar, coconut palm sugar, or maple syrup
- 3 teaspoons of minced garlic
- Tabasco 2 teaspoons, plus extra for serving
- Herbs to garnish, optional

Cooking Instructions:

1. In a medium bowl, add the ground sausage, additional spices and herbs. Use your hands to give everything a good mix.

2. Add the Tabasco sauce and shape them into patties about 3 - 3 1/2 in width and 1 to 1.5 inch thick.

3. Add the formed patties on baking tray lined with parchment paper to avoid sticking. Add about 4-5 patties in the Air Fryer.

4. Cook at 370°F for 20 minutes. Remove the tray when they are half way cooked and turn the patties. Place the stray again into the Air Fryer to continue cooking.

5. Place the sausage on a serving bowl when the timer goes off. Repeat the same procedure for the remaining patties.

6. Serve with extra tabasco sauce or your desired sauce and enjoy!

Coconut Shrimp with Spicy Marmalade Sauce

Preparation time: 10 minutes

Cook time: 20 minutes

Total time: 30 minutes

Servings: 2

Ingredients:

- 8 large shrimp, shelled and deveined
- 8 oz. of coconut milk
- ½ cup of shredded sweetened coconut
- ½ cup of panko bread
- ½ tsp. of cayenne pepper
- ¼ tsp. of kosher salt
- ¼ tsp. of fresh ground pepper
- ½ cup of orange marmalade
- 1 tbsp. of honey
- 1 tsp. of mustard
- ¼ tsp. of hot sauce

Cooking Instructions:

1. Rinse the shrimp and reserve aside.

2. In a medium bowl, whisk together the coconut milk and season with salt and pepper.

3. In another bowl, whisk together the coconut, panko, cayenne pepper, salt and pepper.

4. Place the shrimp in the coconut milk, the panko and then place in the Air Fryer basket. Repeat the same procedure until all the shrimp are coated.

5. Cook the shrimp at 350°F for 20 minutes or until the shrimp are cooked through. Meanwhile, whisk together the marmalade, honey, mustard and hot sauce.

6. Serve with the sauce and enjoy!

Crumbed Fish

Preparation time: 10 minutes

Cook time: 12 minutes

Total time: 22 minutes

Servings: 4

Ingredients:

- 1 cup of dry bread crumbs
- ¼ cup of vegetable oil
- 4 flounder fillets
- 1 egg, beaten
- 1 lemon, sliced

Cooking Instructions:

1. Preheat your Air Fryer to 360°F.

2. In a medium bowl, mix together the breadcrumbs and oil. Give the mixture a good stir to loose and crumble.

3. Place the fish fillets into the egg and remove any excess. Dip fillets into the bread crumb mixture to coat. Place the coated fillet in your Air Fryer.

4. Cook at 360°F for 12 minutes or until the fish flakes easily with a fork. Garnish with lemon slices if desired.

5. Serve and enjoy!

Bang Bang Fried Shrimp

Preparation time: 10 minutes

Cook time: 20 minutes

Total time: 30 minutes

Servings: 4

Ingredients:

- 1 lb. of raw shrimp, peeled and deveined
- 1 egg white 3 tablespoons
- ½ cup of all-purpose flour
- ¾ cup of panko bread crumbs
- 1 teaspoon of paprika
- McCormick's Grill Mates Montreal Chicken Seasoning to taste
- Salt and pepper to taste
- Cooking spray

Bang Bang Sauce:

- 1/3 cup of plain, non-fat Greek yogurt
- 2 tablespoons of Sriracha
- ¼ cup of sweet chili sauce

Cooking Instructions:

1. Preheat your Air Fryer to 400°F. Generously season the shrimp with the seasonings.

2. Add the flour in a bowl, egg whites in another bowl, and panko breadcrumbs in a separate bowl.

3. Dip the shrimp in the flour, then the egg whites, and the panko bread crumbs. Spray the shrimp with cooking spray.

4. Place the shrimp in the Air Fryer basket. Cook for 4 minutes. Remove the basket and turn the shrimp to cook on other side. Cook for another 4 minutes or until crisp.

5. In a medium bowl, combine together all of the bang bang sauce ingredients and give everything a good mix to combine.

6. Serve with the bang bang sauce and enjoy!

Fish and Chips

Preparation time: 10 minutes

Cook time: 35 minutes

Total time: 45 minutes

Servings: 4s

Ingredients:

- 1 pound of fish fillet (cod, tilapia, catfish)
- 1 cup of breadcrumbs (We used panko)
- 1 egg, beaten
- ¼ cup of flour
- 1 teaspoon of salt
- 2 tablespoons of oil
- 2 russet potatoes

Cooking Instructions:

1. In a medium bowl, cut in the potatoes in wedges and add the salt and oil.

2. Place the potatoes in the Air Fryer basket. Cook at 400°F for 20 minutes, shaking twice. When done, remove the potatoes from the basket and set aside.

3. Add the flour in a bowl, add the beaten egg in another bowl, and add the breadcrumbs in a separate bowl.

4. Dip the fish fillet first in flour, then in egg, and then in breadcrumbs. Place the fish in the Air Fryer.

5. Cook at 350°F for 15 minutes. Check on it halfway through and turn the fish to cook on other side.

6. Serve with your desired sauce and enjoy!

Garlic Lime Shrimp Kabobs

Preparation time: 5 minutes

Cook time: 8 minutes

Total time: 13 minutes

Servings: 2

Ingredients:

- 1 cup of raw shrimp
- 1 garlic clove
- 1 lime
- 1/8 tsp. of salt
- Freshly ground pepper
- 5 6 inch wooden skewers

Cooking Instructions:

1. Place the wooden skewer in water to soak for about 20 minutes. Thaw shrimp, if frozen.

2. Preheat your Air fryer to 350°F. In a medium bowl, mix together the shrimp with juiced lime and minced garlic.

3. Season with salt and pepper. Place the shrimp on each skewer. Place in the Air Fryer.

4. Cook for 8 minutes, and turn when they are half way cooked. Top with chopped cilantro and your desired dip.

5. Serve and enjoy!

Bacon Wrapped Filet Mignon

Preparation time: 5 minutes

Cook time: 15 minutes

Total time: 20 minutes

Servings: 2

Ingredients:

- 2 filet mignon steaks
- 2 slices of bacon
- 2 toothpicks
- 1 tsp. of freshly cracked peppercorns
- ½ tsp. of kosher salt
- Avocado oil

Cooking Instructions:

1. First, wrap up the bacon around the filet mignon and press the toothpick through the bacon and into the filet.

2. Press the other toothpick out of the filet into the bacon on the other end of the toothpick. Generously season with the salt and pepper or your desired seasonings.

3. Place the bacon wrapped filet mignon in the Air Fryer basket. Spray the bacon wrapped mignon fillet with a little avocado oil.

4. Cook the steak at 375°F for 10 minutes. Remove the basket and turn the steak to cook on other side for more 5 minutes or until your desired doneness is achieved.

5. Serve and enjoy!

Cajun Salmon

Serves: 1

Ingredients:

- 1 piece fresh salmon fillet (about 200g)
- Cajun seasoning (just enough to coat)
- A light sprinkle of sugar, optional
- Juice from a quarter of lemon

Cooking Instructions:

1. Preheat the Air Fryer to 180°C. Rinse the salmon and pat dry with a paper towel.

2. In a medium bowl, add the salmon fillet and sprinkle with the Cajun seasoning on both sides to coat.

3. Add a light sprinkling of sugar. Place the salmon in the Air Fryer grill pan, with the skin side up.

4. Cook for 7 minutes for a salmon fillet about ¾ inch thick.

5. Serve with a squeeze of lemon and enjoy!

Coconut Shrimp

Preparation time: 10 minutes

Cook time: 20 minutes

Total time: 30 minutes

Servings: 4

Ingredients:

- ½ cup of sweetened coconut flakes
- ½ cup of panko bread crumbs
- ½ teaspoon of salt
- ½ teaspoon of paprika
- ½ teaspoon of garlic powder
- ¼ teaspoon of pepper
- ½ pound of large shrimp, peeled, deveined, tails on
- 1 egg

Cooking Instructions:

1. Preheat your Air Fryer to 400°F. Spray the Air Fryer basket with cooking spray.

2. In a medium bowl, add together the coconut flakes, panko, salt, paprika, garlic powder and pepper and give everything a good stir to combine.

3. In a separate bowl, beat the egg and set aside. Pat the shrimp dry with a paper towel.

4. Dip each of the shrimp in egg, then in the bread crumb mixture until completely coated. Place the coated shrimp in the Air Fryer basket.

5. Cook for about 5 minutes or until cooked through. Repeat the same procedure with the rest of the shrimp.

6. Serve with your desired sauce and enjoy!

Honey-Glazed Salmon

Ingredients:

- 2 pieces of salmon fillets (about 100gm each)
- 6 tablespoons of honey
- 6 teaspoons of soy sauce
- 3 teaspoons of Hon Mirin (or Rice Wine Vinegar)
- 1 teaspoon of water

Cooking Instruction:

1. In a medium bowl, mix together the honey, soy sauce, Hon Mirin or rice wine vinegar and water.

2. In a separate bowl, pour half of the mixture and set aside to serve as sauce.

3. Add the salmon and the marinade mixture and allow to marinate for about 2 hours. Preheat your Air Fryer to 180°C.

4. Cook the salmon for 8 minutes. Turn the salmon when they are half way cooked and cook for another 5 minutes.

5. Pour the marinade mixture over the salmon every 3 minutes. Pour the rest of the sauce in a pan and allow to simmer for 1 minutes to make the sauce.

6. Serve with salmon and enjoy!

Cajun Shrimp

Serves: 2

Ingredients:

- ½ lb. of tiger shrimp (16-20 count)
- ¼ tsp. of cayenne pepper
- ½ tsp. of old bay seasoning
- ¼ tsp. of smoked paprika
- 1 pinch of salt
- 1 tbsp. of olive oil

Cooking Instructions:

1. Preheat your Air Fryer to 390°F.

2. In a medium bowl, combine together all of the ingredients and give everything a good mix to combine.

3. Coat the shrimp with the mixture containing oil and the spices.

4. Place the shrimp into the Air Fryer basket. Cook for 5 minutes.

5. Serve over rice and enjoy!

Tomato Mayonnaise Shrimp

Preparation time: 5 minutes

Cook time: 8 minutes

Total time: 13 minutes

Servings: 4

Ingredients:

- 1 lb. of large 21-25 count peeled, tail-on shrimp
- 3 tbsp. of mayonnaise
- 1 tbsp. of ketchup
- 1 tbsp. of minced garlic
- 1 tsp. of sriracha
- ½ tsp. of smoked paprika
- ½ tsp. of salt

For Finishing:

- ½ cup of chopped green onions green and white parts

Cooking Instructions:

1. In a mixing bowl, add together the mayo, ketchup, garlic, sriracha, paprika, and salt and give everything a good mix to combine.

2. Add the shrimp to the sauce and toss to coat with the mixture. Spray your Air Fryer basket with oil.

3. Place the shrimp into the Air Fryer basket. Cook at 325°F for 8 minutes or until shrimp are cooked, flip the shrimp half way through and spraying with oil again.

4. Sprinkle with chopped onions and serve immediately.

AIR FRYER BEEF & PORK RECIPES

Pork Chops

Preparation time: 2 minutes

Cook time: 10 minutes

Total time: 12 minutes

Servings: 2

Ingredients:

- 2 pork chops
- 2 cups of pork rinds
- 2 tablespoons of pork fat
- Salt & Pepper

Cooking Instructions:

1. Preheat your Air Fryer to 180°C/360°F.

2. Add the pork chops on a cutting board and sprinkle with salt and pepper.

3. Brush pork fat over the pork chops to coat it and place them with the pork rinds in the Air Fryer basket.

4. Cook at 180°C/360°F for 10 minutes.

5. Serve and enjoy!

Beef Empanadas

Preparation time: 10 minutes

Cook time: 16 minutes

Total time: 26 minutes

Ingredients:

- 8 Goya empanada discs, thawed
- 1 cup of picadillo
- 1 egg white, whisked
- 1 tsp. of water

Cooking Instructions:

1. Preheat for 8 minutes at 325°F. Spray your Air Fryer basket with cooking spray.

2. Add 2 tablespoons of picadillo in the middle of each disc. Fold in half and press the edges with a fork.

3. Repeat the same procedures with the rest of the dough. Whisk the egg whites with water and brush the tops of the empanadas.

4. Place in the Air Fryer. Bake in batches, about 2 or 3 at a time for 8 minutes, or until golden.

5. Remove from the Air Fryer and repeat the same procedure with the rest of the empanadas.

6. Serve and enjoy!

Stromboli

Servings: 4

Ingredients:

- 12 oz. of pizza crust, refrigerated
- 3 cups of cheddar cheese, shredded
- 0.75 cup of Mozzarella cheese, shredded
- 0.333333 lb. of cooked ham, sliced
- 3 oz. of red bell peppers, roasted
- 1 egg yolk
- 1 tbsp. of milk

Cooking Instructions:

1. Roll the dough to form about ¼ inch thick and layer the ham.

2. Add the cheese and peppers on one side of the dough. Fold over and press with a fork to seal.

3. In a medium bowl, mix together the egg and milk and brush the dough. Add the Stromboli into the Air Fryer basket.

4. Cook at 360°F for 15 minutes. Flip the Stromboli every 5 minutes to cook on other side.

5. Serve and enjoy!

Roasted Stuffed Peppers

Ingredients:

- 2 medium green peppers, stems and seeds removed, and cook for 3 minutes in boiling salted water
- ½ small onion, chopped
- 1 clove garlic, minced
- 1 tsp. of olive oil
- 8 oz. of lean ground beef
- ½ cup of tomato sauce
- 1 tsp. of Worcestershire sauce
- ½ tsp. of salt
- ½ tsp. of black pepper
- 4 oz. of cheddar cheese, shredded

Cooking Instructions:

1. Preheat the Air Fryer to 390°F.

2. In a nonstick pan, add the olive oil and brown the onion and garlic until golden.

3. In a medium bowl, blend the beef, cooked vegetables, ¼ cup tomato sauce, Worcestershire, salt and pepper and half the shredded cheese.

4. Divide and stuff the pepper halves and top with the rest of the tomato sauce and cheese.

5. Layer in the Air Fryer basket. Bake for about 15 to 20 minutes or until the meat is cooked.

6. Serve and enjoy!

Rib Eye Steak

Servings: 4

Ingredients:

- 2 lb. of rib eye steak
- 1 tbsp. of steak rub
- 1 tbsp. of olive oil

Cooking Instructions:

1. Preheat the Air Fryer to 400°F.

2. Generously season the steak on each side with olive oil.

3. Place steak in the Air Fryer basket. Cook at 400°F for 14 minutes.

4. Flip the steak every 7 minutes to cook on other side.

5. Remove the steak from the Air Fryer basket and slice before serving.

6. Serve and enjoy!

Pork Taquitos

Servings: 10

Ingredients:

- 3 cups of cooked shredded pork tenderloin or chicken
- 2 ½ cups of fat free shredded mozzarella
- 10 small flour tortillas
- 1 lime, juiced
- Cooking spray

Cooking Instructions:

1. Preheat your Air Fryer to 380°F. Sprinkle lime juice over pork and rub them to coat.

2. Add 5 tortillas in your microwave 5 and heat for 10 seconds, to soften. Add 3 ounces of pork and ¼ cup of cheese to a tortilla.

3. Roll up the tortillas and lay the tortillas on a greased foil lined pan. Spray the tortillas with cooking spray to coat.

4. Place in the Air Fryer and cook for about 7-10 minutes at 380°F or until tortillas are a golden color.

5. Turn the tortillas when they are half way cooked to cook on other side.

6. Serve and enjoy!

Beef Hotpot

Preparation time: 5 minutes

Cook time: 19 minutes

Total time: 24 minutes

Servings: 4

Ingredients:

- Leftover Stew we used leftover Cornish pasty mix
- 4 large carrots, peeled and diced
- 4 small potatoes, peeled and diced
- Beef gravy granules
- 1 teaspoon of olive oil
- Salt & Pepper

Cooking Instructions:

1. Add the diced carrots into the bottom of your Instant Pot and pour 250ml of warm water.

2. Close and lock the lid in place. Select Manual, High Pressure for 4 minutes. In a medium bowl, mix together the salt, pepper and a teaspoon of olive oil with your hands.

3. Place in Air Fryer and cook at 160°C/320°F for 10 minutes. Cook for additional 200°C/400°F for 5 minutes.

4. When the timer beeps, do a natural pressure release for about 10 minutes. Carefully open the lid and add the stew leftovers.

5. Add in the beef gravy granules and give everything a good stir. Select the Sauté function and simmer to thicken the liquid.

6. Add the filling and the air fried potatoes on top.

7. Serve warm and enjoy!

Country Fried Steak

Servings: 1

Ingredients:

- 6 oz. of sirloin steak-pounded thin
- 3 eggs, beaten
- 1 cup of flour
- 1 cup of Panko
- 1 tsp. of onion powder
- 1 tsp. of garlic powder
- 1 tsp. of salt
- 1 tsp. of pepper
- 6 oz. of ground sausage meat
- 2 tbsp. of flour
- 2 cup of milk
- 1 tsp. of pepper

Cooking Instructions:

1. Generously season the panko with the spices.

2. Dip the steak flour, in the egg, and seasoned panko. Add the breaded steak into the Air Fryer basket.

3. Cook at 370°F for 12 minutes. Remove the steak from the basket and serve with mash potatoes and sausage gravy.

4. Cook the sausage in a pan, until well done. Remove the fat, and set 2 tablespoons of fat aside in the pan.

5. Add in the flour to the pan with sausage, and give everything a good mix to incorporate the flour.

6. Mix in the milk and cook over a medium heat to thicken the milk. Season with salt and pepper.

7. Cook for about 3 minutes to cook out the flour.

8. Serve and enjoy!

Pork Rinds

Preparation time: 2 minutes

Cook time: 10 minutes

Total time: 12 minutes

Servings: 1

Ingredients:

- 1 Kilo Pork Belly, diced into small cubes

Cooking Instructions:

1. Trim the fat layer from the pork belly and dice the pork belly fat into small cubes.

2. Add the pork belly into the Air Fryer baking pan. Cook for 10 minutes at 200°C/400°F.

3. Pat the pork fat dry with kitchen towel. Refrigerate the pork fat for about 10 minutes to cool down.

4. Blend the pork fat in your blender until it looks like coarse bread crumbs.

5. Serve and enjoy!

Taco Bell Crunch Wraps

Servings: 6

Preparation time: 15 minutes

Cook time: 4 minutes

Total time: 19 minutes

Ingredients:

- 2 pounds of ground beef
- 2 servings of Homemade Taco Seasoning Recipe
- 1 1/3 cup of water
- 6 flour tortillas, 12 inch
- 3 roma tomatoes
- 12 ounces of nacho cheese
- 2 cups of lettuce, shredded
- 2 cups of Mexican blend cheese
- 2 cups of sour cream
- 6 tostadas
- Olive oil or butter spray

Cooking Instructions:

1. Preheat your Air Fryer to 400°F. Prepare your ground beef according to the instructions on the taco seasoning packet.

2. Add the following ingredients in the center of each flour tortilla: 2/3 cup of beef, 4 tablespoons of nacho cheese, 1 tostada, and 1/3 cup of sour cream.

3. Add the 1/3 cup of lettuce. 1/6th of the tomatoes and 1/3 cup of cheese. Fold the edges up, over the center and press with a fork to close.

4. Repeat the same procedure with the rest of the wraps. Arrange them up, side down in the Air Fryer basket. Spray the wraps with oil.

5. Cook for 2 minutes or until brown. Turn the wraps with a spatula when they are half way cooked and spray with oil again.

6. Cook another 2 minutes and repeat with rest of the wraps. Allow to cool for a couple of minutes.

7. Serve and enjoy!

AIR FRYER EGG RECIPES

Egg Rolls

Preparation time: 30 minutes

Cook time: 15 minutes

Total time: 45 minutes

Servings: 16

Ingredients:

- 2 cups of frozen corn, thawed
- 1 (15 oz.) can black beans, drained and rinsed
- 1 (13.5 oz.) can spinach, drained
- 1 ½ cups of shredded jalapeno Jack cheese
- 1 cup of sharp Cheddar cheese, shredded
- 1 (4 oz.) can diced green chilies, drained
- 4 green onions, sliced
- 1 tsp. of salt
- 1 tsp. of ground cumin
- 1 tsp. of chili powder
- 1 (16 oz.) package egg roll wrappers
- Cooking spray

Cooking Instructions:

1. In a medium bowl, mix together the corn, beans, spinach, jalapeno Jack cheese, Cheddar cheese, and green chilies.

2. Add the green onions, salt, cumin, and chili powder and give everything a good mix to make the filling. Lay an egg roll wrapper at an angle.

3. Moisten all 4 edges with water using your hands. Add about ¼ cup of the filling in the center of the wrapper. Roll up the sides over filling.

4. Repeat the procedure with the rest of the wrappers. Spray each of the egg roll with cooking spray. Preheat the Air Fryer to 390°F (199°C).

5. Add the egg rolls in the Air Fryer basket. Cook for 8 minutes, cooking in batches if desired.

6. Turn the eggs and cook for additional 4 minutes or until skins are crispy. Serve and enjoy!

Puffed Egg Tarts

Ingredients:

- All-purpose flour
- 1 sheet frozen puff pastry half a 17.3-oz/490 g package, thawed
- 3/4 cup of shredded cheese such as Gruyere, Cheddar or Monterey Jack, divided
- 4 large eggs
- 1 tablespoon of minced fresh parsley or chives, optional

Cooking Instructions:

1. Preheat the Air Fryer to 390°F (200°C). Unfold the pastry sheet on a flat board and cut them into 4 squares.

2. Add 2 squares in Air Fryer basket. Cook for 10 minutes or until golden brown. Remove the basket and press down the centers of each squares with a metal spoon.

3. Sprinkle with 3 tablespoons of cheese into each hole in the center and crack an egg into the center of each pastry.

4. Cook for about 7 to 11 minutes or until eggs are cooked to your preferred doneness. Place the eggs on a wire rack and allow to cool for about 5 minutes.

5. Sprinkle with half the parsley, if desired. Repeat the same procedures with the rest of the pastry squares, cheese, eggs and parsley.

6. Serve warm and enjoy!

Easy Breakfast Sandwich

Servings: 1

Ingredients:

- 1 free range egg
- 1 English bacon or 2 streaky bacons
- 1 English muffin
- Pinch of pepper
- Pinch of salt

Cooking Instructions:

1. In a heatproof bowl, crack the egg into the bowl.

2. Place the egg, bacon and muffin into the Air Fryer basket.

3. Cook for about 6 minutes at 392°F (200°C).

4. Serve and enjoy!

Avocado Egg Boat

Preparation time: 1 minutes

Cook time: 8 minutes

Total time: 9 minutes

Servings: 2

Ingredients:

- 2 medium avocados, sliced in half
- 4 medium eggs
- Fresh parsley
- Fresh chives
- Salt & pepper

Cooking Instructions:

1. Remove the stones and remove about 20% of the flesh.
2. Season them with salt, pepper, fresh parsley and chives.
3. Crack an egg into each of the four halves and add in the Air Fryer basket.
4. Cook at 175°C for 8 minutes. Sprinkle with extra fresh parsley, more salt and pepper.
5. Serve and enjoy!

Hard Boiled Eggs

Preparation time: 2 minutes

Cook time: 15 minutes

Total time: 17 minutes

Servings: 6

Ingredients:

- 6 eggs

Cooking Instructions:

1. Place the eggs in the Air Fryer rack.

2. Cook at 260°F for 15 minutes. Remove the eggs and into an ice water bath for 10 minutes.

3. Serve and enjoy!

Baked Eggs

Ingredients:

- 1 egg
- Non-stick cooking spray
- Seasonings

Cooking Instructions:

1. Preheat the Air Fryer to 180°F.
2. Spray the ramekin with nonstick cooking spray.
3. Crack an egg into your ramekin. Season with salt and pepper.
4. Bake at 330°F for 5 minutes.
5. Serve and enjoy!

Breakfast Soufflé

Servings: 4

Ingredients:

- 4 eggs
- 4 tbsp. of light cream
- Red chili pepper, chopped
- Parsley, chopped

Cooking Instructions:

1. In a medium bowl, crack the egg and stir in the cream, parsley and pepper.
2. Add the egg mixture to fill the dishes up to halfway.
3. Bake at 392°F (200°C) for 8 minutes. Cook for additional 5 minutes.
4. Serve and enjoy!

Scrambled Eggs

Preparation time: 1 minute

Cook time: 9 minutes

Total time: 10 minutes

Servings: 2

Ingredients:

- 2 Slices Whole meal bread
- 4 large eggs
- Pinch of salt
- Pinch of pepper

Cooking Instructions:

1. Warm the bread for about 3 minutes at 200°C/400°F.
2. Crack the eggs into a baking pan and give everything a good stir.
3. Add the seasoning and add the baking pan in to your Air Fryer.
4. Cook for 2 minutes at 180°C/360°F.
5. Cook for additional 4 minutes. Pour the scrambled eggs over the whole meal toast.
6. Serve and enjoy!

Frozen Egg Rolls

Preparation time: 4 minutes

Cook time: 16 minutes

Total time: 16 minutes

Servings: 4

Ingredients:

- Pack Frozen Egg Rolls
- 1 medium egg

Cooking Instructions:

1. In a medium bowl, crack the egg and beat it with a fork.
2. Using a pastry brush, brush the tops of your egg rolls with egg to coat the frozen egg.
3. Place in the Air Fryer grill pan. Cook at 160°C/320°F for 8 minutes.
4. Flip the frozen egg rolls over and brush the other side with more egg.
5. Cook for additional 8 minutes at 160°C/320°F.
6. Serve warm and enjoy!

Easy Omelette

Ingredients:

- 2 eggs
- ¼ cup of milk
- Pinch of salt
- Fresh meat and veggies, diced
- 1 tsp. of McCormick Good Morning Breakfast Seasoning – Garden Herb
- ¼ cup of shredded cheese (We used cheddar and mozzarella)

Cooking Instructions:

1. In a medium bowl, mix together the eggs and milk and give everything a good stir to combine.

2. Add a pinch of salt, and your veggies to the egg mixture. Pour the egg mixture into a well-greased and place the pan into your Air Fryer basket.

3. Cook at 350°F for 8-10 minutes. Flip the eggs when they are half way cooked and sprinkle with breakfast seasoning onto the eggs.

4. Sprinkle the cheese over the top. Loosen the edges of the egg from the pan with a wooden spatula and transfer to a serving place.

5. Garnish with extra green onions, if desired and serve immediately.

Chicken Egg Rolls

Ingredients:

- 12 ½ ounces chunk chicken breast, canned and drained
- 6 egg roll wrappers
- 16 ounces of packaged coleslaw mix
- 1 egg, beaten
- ¼ cup of low sodium soy sauce
- 1 teaspoon of minced garlic
- Spray oil
- 1 teaspoon of ground ginger
- 1 teaspoon of sugar

Cooking Instructions:

1. In a medium bowl, mix together the soy sauce, garlic, ginger, and sugar.

2. Fold in chicken and coleslaw and give everything a good mix to combine. Lay 1 egg roll wrapper and fill with 3 tablespoons of the mixture.

3. Fold bottom point up over filling and roll once. Fold in and press right and left points with a fork. Brush the top point with beaten egg and finish rolling.

4. Repeat the procedure with the remaining ingredients until all 6 rolls are done. Place the egg rolls into the Air Fryer basket.

5. Spray egg rolls with oil. Cook for 8 to 10 minutes at 390°F, flipping half way through to cook on other side.

6. Serve and enjoy!

Baked Eggs in Bread Bowls

Servings: 4

Ingredients:

- 4 crusty dinner rolls
- 4 eggs, large
- 4 tbsp. of mixed herbs, chopped (parsley, chives, tarragon)
- 4 tbsp. of heavy cream
- Salt and pepper
- Parmesan cheese, grated

Cooking Instructions:

1. Slice off top of each dinner roll and remove some bread to create a hole to place the egg.

2. Layer the dinner rolls on a baking sheet and set the tops aside. Crack an egg into each roll.

3. Top each egg with few herbs and a little bit cream. Season with salt and pepper. Sprinkle with Parmesan.

4. Place in the Air Fryer. Bake at a 350°F (180°C) for 20 to 25 minutes or until eggs are set and bread is toasted.

5. When the eggs have cooked for about 20 minutes, add the bread tops on baking sheet and bake until golden brown.

6. Allow to rest for about 5 minutes. Place tops on rolls.

7. Serve warm and enjoy!

Bacon & Eggs

Preparation time: 1 minute

Cook time: 13 minutes

Total time: 14 minutes

Servings: 4

Ingredients:

- 4 ramekins
- 8 Back Bacon
- 4 large eggs
- Fresh chives, optional
- Salt & Pepper

Cooking Instructions:

1. Place the bacon around the sides and bottom of ramekins.

2. Crack an egg into the center of each ramekin.

3. Place in the Air Fryer. Cook at 180°C for 13 minutes.

4. Season with salt and pepper and fresh chives.

5. Serve and enjoy!

Cheese and Veggie Egg Cups

Preparation time: 10 minutes

Cook time: 20 minutes

Total time: 30 minutes

Servings: 4

Ingredients:

- 4 large eggs
- 1 cup of diced veggies of choice
- 1 cup of shredded cheese
- 4 tablespoons of half and half
- 1 tablespoon of chopped cilantro
- Salt and Pepper

Cooking Instructions:

1. Grease 4 ramekins. In a medium bowl, whisk together the eggs, vegetables, half the cheese, and half and half.

2. Add the cilantro, and salt and pepper. Divide the ingredients among the 4 ramekins. Place ramekins in the Air Fryer basket.

3. Cook at 300°F for 12 minutes. Top the cups with remaining cheese.

4. Cook at 400°F for additional 2 minutes or until cheese is melted and browned.

5. Serve warm and enjoy!

Easy Full English

Servings: 4

Ingredients:

- 8 paper muffin cases
- 1 small egg
- 2 tbsp. of vegetable oil
- (75ml) milk
- 3½ ounces (100g) plain flour
- 1 tbsp. of baking powder
- Pinch mustard powder
- 1½ oz. (40g) Parmesan, grated
- Dash of Worcestershire sauce

Cooking Instructions:

1. Preheat the Air Fryer to 392°F (200°C). Add up the muffin cases to become four.

2. In a medium bowl, beat the egg, add the oil and milk, flour, baking powder and mustard.

3. Give everything a good mix until smooth. Stir in the cheese and Worcestershire sauce.

4. Ladle the batter into the cases and place in the Air Fryer basket.

5. Bake at 392°F for 15 minutes or until golden.

6. Serve and enjoy!

AIR FRYER SIDE DISH RECIPES

Pizza Hut Bread Sticks

Preparation time: 10 minutes

Cook time: 15 minutes

Total time: 25 minutes

Servings: 4

Ingredients:

- 1/3 Homemade Pizza Dough
- 2 tablespoons of desiccated coconut
- 1 teaspoon of garlic puree
- 25 g of cheddar cheese
- Bread seeds, optional
- 1 teaspoon of parsley
- Salt & Pepper

Cooking Instructions:

1. Add the oil in a small pan and heat on a medium heat to melt.

2. Pour the melted oil to the seasoning and your garlic puree. Give everything a good mix and roll out your pizza dough.

3. Form the shapes into a thick rectangular shape. Cover it with your garlic oil to coat using a baking brush.

4. Sprinkle the top with the desiccated coconut until the garlic oil is no longer visible. Add an extra sprinkle of cheddar cheese and finish with some bread seeds.

5. Place in the Air Fryer basket. Cook at 180°C for 10 minutes. Cook for additional 5 minutes at 200°C or until crispy. When done, chop into fingers.

6. Serve and enjoy!

Sloppy Joes Stuffed Cheese Scones

Preparation time: 15 minutes

Cook time: 20 minutes

Total time: 35 minutes

Servings: 4

Ingredients:

- 50 g of sloppy joes
- 175 g of Self Raising flour
- 25 g of butter
- 25 g of cheddar cheese, grated
- 4 cheese slices
- 1 medium egg
- 5 tablespoons of oregano
- Salt & Pepper

Cooking Instructions:

1. Make the scones. In a medium bowl, mix together all the seasoning, flour and your butter.

2. Rub the butter into the flour until it looks like breadcrumbs. Add the grated cheese, egg and milk. Give everything a good mix to combine into a dough mixture.

3. Add little milk if the mixture is too hard until it is a soft dough. Divide the mixture into 4 sized scone shapes.

4. Place in the Air Fryer basket. Bake at 160°C for 15 minutes. Remove them and place on a cooling rack to cool.

5. Slice the top with a knife and remove the bulk of the center. Mix the spare center with the sloppy joes and ladle the mixture into the scones.

6. Add the lids on top followed by a slice of cheese. Place back in the Air Fryer basket. Cook for additional 5 minutes.

7. Serve and enjoy!

Garlic Potatoes

Preparation time: 5 minutes

Cook time: 20 minutes

Total time: 25 minutes

Servings: 2

Ingredients:

- 3 rashers unsmoked bacon, diced
- 6 medium potatoes, peeled and chopped
- 1 teaspoon of garlic puree
- 2 teaspoons of olive oil
- Salt & Pepper

Cooking Instructions:

1. Peel and chop the potatoes into medium sized cubes.

2. Place the potatoes in the Air Fryer basket and add 1 tsp. of olive oil. Cook at 180°C for 10 minutes.

3. Meanwhile, dice your bacon in a medium bowl. Add the garlic, extra teaspoon of olive oil and salt and pepper and give everything a good mix.

4. Add the potatoes to the bowl and give everything a good mix. Place the potatoes and bacon mixture on a sheet of silver foil.

5. Cut the sheet of silver foil and cook for additional 10 minutes at 180°C.

6. Serve and enjoy!

Courgette Fritters

Preparation time: 10 minutes

Cook time: 15 minutes

Total time: 25 minutes

Servings: 9

Ingredients:

- 100 g of plain flour
- 1 small egg, beaten
- 5 tablespoons of milk
- 150 g of grated courgette
- 75 g of onion, peeled and diced
- 25 g of cheddar cheese, grated
- 1 tablespoon of mixed herbs
- Salt & Pepper

Cooking Instructions:

1. In a medium bowl, add the plain flour and add the seasoning.

2. Whisk together the egg and milk. Add the mixture to the flour to make a smooth creamy batter.

3. Grate the courgette and ensure that any excess moisture is removed. Add the onion and stir in the cheese.

4. Add extra flour and cheese to thicken the batter if the mixture isn't very thick.

5. Use your hands to make them into small burger shapes. Place them in your Air Fryer basket.

6. Cook at 200°C for 20 minutes or until fully cooked. Serve with a good dollop of sour cream or mayonnaise if desired and enjoy!

Air Fryer Croutons

Preparation time: 3 minutes

Cook time: 8 minutes

Total time: 11 minutes

Servings: 9

Ingredients:

- 2 slices of whole meal bread, chopped into medium chunks
- 1 tablespoon of olive oil

Cooking Instructions:

1. Chop the slices of whole meal bread into medium chunks.
2. Place the chunks of bread into the Air Fryer basket.
3. Add the 1 tablespoon of olive oil. Cook at 200°C for 8 minutes.
4. Serve over soup or as a snack if desired and enjoy!

Cheese Pull Apart Bread

Preparation time: 15 minutes

Cook time: 4 minutes

Total time: 19 minutes

Servings: 2

Ingredients:

- 1 large bread loaf
- 100 g of butter
- 2 teaspoons of garlic puree
- 30 g of cheddar cheese
- 30 g of goats cheese
- 30 g of mozzarella cheese
- 30 g of soft cheese
- 30 g edam cheese
- 2 teaspoons of chives
- Salt & Pepper

Cooking Instructions:

1. Grate the hard cheese into 4 different piles and set aside.

2. Add the butter in a sauce pan and heat over medium heat to melt. Add the chives, salt and pepper and the garlic.

3. Cook for additional 2 minutes. Give everything a good mix and set aside. Make little holes into the bread with a bread knife.

4. Fill each of the little slit wholes with the garlic butter. Cover all them with soft cheese to provide a creamy taste.

5. Add a little cheddar and a little goats' cheese on every other side. Add the Edam and mozzarella to ones that are not filled.

6. Place in the Air Fryer basket. Cook for about 4 minutes or until the cheese is melted and the bread is warm. Remove from the Air Fryer and place on a cooling rack.

7. Serve and enjoy!

Stuffed Garlic Mushrooms

Preparation time: 10 minutes

Cook time: 25 minutes

Total time: 35 minutes

Servings: 4

Ingredients:

- 6 of medium mushrooms
- 20 g of onion, peeled and diced
- 1 tablespoon of breadcrumbs
- 1 teaspoon of garlic puree
- 1 tablespoon of olive oil
- 1 teaspoon of parsley
- Salt & Pepper

Cooking Instructions:

1. In a medium bowl, mix together the breadcrumbs, olive oil, garlic, onion, parsley, salt and pepper.

2. Give everything a good mix. Rinse the mushrooms and remove the middle stalks.

3. Add the breadcrumb mixture to fill the center. Cook at 180°C for 10 minutes.

4. Serve and enjoy!

Sage & Onion Stuffing Balls

Preparation time: 3 minutes

Cook time: 15 minutes

Total time: 18 minutes

Servings: 9

Ingredients:

- 100 g of sausage meat
- ½ medium onion, peeled and diced
- ½ teaspoon of garlic puree
- 1 teaspoon of sage
- 3 tablespoons of breadcrumbs
- Salt & Pepper

Cooking Instructions:

1. In a medium bowl, add together all of the ingredients and give everything a good mix.

2. Form the mixture into medium sized balls. Place them in your Air Fryer basket.

3. Cook for 15 minutes at 180°C. Remove them from the Air Fryer.

4. Serve and enjoy!

Pigs In Blankets

Preparation time: 3 minutes

Cook time: 15 minutes

Total time: 18 minutes

Servings: 9

Ingredients:

- 9 Back Bacon
- 3 large Brazilian sausages, chopped into three equal sizes
- Salt & Pepper

Cooking Instructions:

1. Chop the sausages into three equal sizes.

2. Wrap the sausages in the bacon to enable each piece of sausage to have one rasher of bacon.

3. Place them in your Air Fryer basket. Cook at 180°C for 15 minutes. Season with salt and pepper.

4. Serve and enjoy!

AIR FRYER BURGER RECIPES

Double Cheese Burger

Preparation time: 5 minutes

Cook time: 22 minutes

Total time: 27 minutes

Servings: 4

Ingredients:

- 4 Burger Buns
- 500 g of pork, minced
- 1 medium onion, diced
- ½ medium Onion, peeled and sliced
- 100 g of cheddar cheese
- 1 tablespoon of soft cheese
- Pinch of salt
- Pinch of pepper

Cooking Instructions:

1. In a medium bowl, add together the mince, diced onion, seasoning and the soft cheese.

2. Give everything a good mix to form a big ball of meat. Divide the meat into 8 even sized burgers. Place the 4 burgers into your Air Fryer.

3. Cook at 180°C for 10 minutes. Remove the burgers and place them on a baking tray. Sprinkle the top with cheese.

4. Place them in the oven on low for 10 minutes while the remaining batch of burgers is cooking in your Air Fryer.

5. Add the sliced onion with a little olive oil in the saucepan and sauté when the last burger is remaining about 5 minutes to be done.

6. When the burgers are done, garnish with salad at the bottom of the bun with a burger on top and then press the other burger on top with a fork.

7. Sprinkle with some more cheese along with some fried onion. Serve with fries and homemade sauce if desired and enjoy.

Bunless Burgers

Preparation time: 5 minutes

Cook time: 20 minutes

Total time: 25 minutes

Servings: 4

Ingredients:

- 400 g of minced beef
- 1 medium red onion, peeled and diced
- 1 small avocado, peeled and diced
- 3 small tomatoes, diced
- 4 slices back bacon
- 1 tablespoon of tomato puree
- 1 tablespoon of olive oil
- Handful green beans
- Handful lettuce
- Handful fresh thyme
- Handful fresh basil
- 1 tablespoon of parsley
- Salt & Pepper

Cooking Instructions:

1. Preheat your Air Fryer to 180°C. Rinse and dice your fresh herbs. Peel and slice the avocado.

2. Dice the red onion and fresh tomato. In a medium bowl, add together the minced beef, 1/5 of the red onion, all the seasonings, and tomato puree.

3. Give everything a good mix and form them into 4 burger shapes. Place the baking mat at the bottom of your Air Fryer.

4. Place the burgers onto the baking sheet. Cook at 180°C for 10 minutes. Add the green beans in the olive oil after 10 minutes and place in the Air Fryer with burgers.

5. Cook for additional 5 minutes and add the slices of bacon. Cook for more 5 minutes.

6. Place the burgers in a serving bowl with the burgers with the green beans, avocado, bacon and salad garnish. Serve and enjoy!

Veggie Burgers

Preparation time: 6 minutes

Cook time: 25 minutes

Total time: 31 minutes

Servings: 6

Ingredients:

- 500 g of sweet potato
- 800 g of cauliflower
- 190 g of carrots
- 1 cup of chickpeas
- 2 cups whole meal breadcrumbs
- 1 cup of grated mozzarella cheese
- 1 tablespoon of mixed herbs
- 1 tablespoon of basil
- Salt & Pepper

Cooking Instructions:

1. Peel and chop your vegetables. Add your chopped vegetables into the bottom of your Instant Pot.

2. Pour 1 cup of warm water into the pot. Close and lock the lid in place and ensure that the valve is in sealing position.

3. Select Manual, High Pressure for 10 minutes. When the timer beeps, do a quick pressure release. Carefully open the lid and drain the vegetables.

4. Squeeze out any excess moisture with a tea towel. Add the chickpeas and mash the vegetables together. Add the breadcrumbs and give everything a good mix.

5. Add the seasonings and make them into veggie burger shapes. Roll in the grated cheese to coat with cheese. Place the veggie burgers in your Air Fryer.

6. Cook at 180°C/360°F for 10 minutes. Cook for additional 5 minutes at the same temperature to get a crusty veggie burger texture.

7. Serve warm in bread buns or with a salad and enjoy!

Turkey Burgers

Preparation time: 2 minutes

Cook time: 20 minutes

Total time: 22 minutes

Servings: 12

Ingredients:

- 500 g of roast dinner leftovers
- 100 g of cheddar cheese
- 100 g of gluten free oats

Cooking Instructions:

1. Preheat your Air Fryer to 180°C.

2. In a medium bowl, add together the leftovers, oats and cheese. Give everything a good mix until combined.

3. Place them in your Air Fryer. Cook at 180°C for 20 minutes. Place on a serving bowl and top with fried egg.

4. Serve and enjoy!

Falafel Burger

Preparation time: 3 minutes

Cook time: 15 minutes

Total time: 18 minutes

Servings: 2

Ingredients:

- 400 g can of chickpeas
- 1 medium red onion
- 1 medium lemon
- 140 g of gluten free oats
- 28 g of cheese
- 28 g of feta cheese
- 3 tablespoons of Greek yoghurt
- 4 tablespoons of soft cheese
- 1 tablespoon of garlic puree
- 1 tablespoon of coriander
- 1 tablespoon of oregano
- 1 tablespoon of parsley
- Salt & Pepper

Cooking Instructions:

1. Add all the seasonings like garlic, lemon rind, red onion, and the drained chickpeas in your food processor or blender.

2. Blend until they are coarse but not smooth. Mix everything in a medium bowl with ½ the soft cheese, the hard cheese and the feta.

3. Make them into burger shapes. Roll them in gluten free oats until the chickpea mixture is no longer seen. Place them in the Air Fryer baking pan.

4. Cook at 180°C/360°F for 8 minutes. Make the burger sauce. In a separate mixing bowl, add the remaining soft cheese, Greek yoghurt and more salt and pepper.

5. Give everything a good mix until it is nice and fluffy. Add the juice of the lemon and give everything a good mix again.

6. Place the falafel burger inside your homemade buns with garnish. Load up with your burger sauce. Serve and enjoy!

Lentil Burgers

Preparation time: 10 minutes

Cook time: 30 minutes

Total time: 40 minutes

Servings: 4

Ingredients:

- 4 vegan burger buns
- 100 g of black beluga lentils
- 1 large carrot, peeled and grated
- 1 medium onion, peeled and diced
- 100 g of white cabbage
- 300 g of gluten free oats
- 1 tablespoon of garlic puree
- 1 teaspoon of cumin
- Handful Fresh Basil, cleaned and chopped
- Salt & Pepper

Cooking Instructions:

1. Blend the gluten free oats in your blender. Blitz until it looks like flour.

2. Add the lentils in a saucepan and pour enough water to cover. Cook on a medium heat for 45 minutes.

3. Place your vegetables into the bottom of your Instant Pot. Close and lock the lid in place. Select the Steam button to cook for 5 minutes.

4. When the timer beeps, d a quick pressure release. Carefully remove the lid and drain the lentils. Place the lentils in a bowl with the steamed vegetables and the oats.

5. Add the seasoning and form them into burgers. Place the burgers in your Air Fryer. Cook at 180°C for 30 minutes.

6. Serve with salad garnish and vegan mayonnaise.

Hamburgers

Preparation time: 3 minutes

Cook time: 17 minutes

Total time: 20 minutes

Servings: 2

Ingredients:

- 2 whole wheat dinner rolls
- 320 g of mixed mince
- 2 medium potatoes, peeled and sliced
- 2 slices of mozzarella cheese
- ¼ medium onion, peeled and diced
- ½ teaspoon of olive oil
- 2 teaspoons of mixed herbs
- 1 teaspoon of mustard
- Salt & Pepper

Cooking Instructions:

1. Peel and slice the potatoes into French Fries. Mix them in ½ tsp. of olive oil and set aside. Peel and dice the onion.

2. In a medium bowl, add the mince, sliced onion and the seasonings and give everything a good mix.

3. Make them into hamburger patty shapes and Place them one side in your Air Fryer. Add the French Fries to the other side.

4. Cook at 180°C/360°F for 15 minutes. Add a slice of mozzarella cheese to the tops of both burgers.

5. Cook for additional 2 minutes at 160°C/320°F for the cheese to melt. Place them inside whole wheat bread buns.

6. Serve and enjoy!

Lamb Burgers

Preparation time: 3 minutes

Cook time: 18 minutes

Total time: 21 minutes

Servings: 4

Ingredients:

Lamb Burgers:

- 650 g of minced lamb
- 2 teaspoons of garlic puree
- 1 teaspoon of Harissa paste
- 1 tablespoon of Moroccan spice
- Salt & Pepper

Greek Dip:

- 3 tablespoons of Greek yoghurt
- 1 teaspoon of Moroccan spice
- ½ teaspoon of oregano
- 1 medium Lemon juice only

Cooking Instructions:

1. In a medium bowl, add all the lamb burger ingredients and give everything a good mix to season the all the lamb mince.

2. Using a burger press, make the mince mixture into lamb burger shapes. Place the lamb burgers in your Air Fryer.

3. Cook at 180°C/360°F for 18 minutes. Meanwhile, make your Greek Dip. Using a fork, mix together Greek dip ingredients.

4. Serve the Greek dip ingredients with your lamb burgers.

Mediterranean Burgers

Preparation time: 3 minutes

Cook time: 15 minutes

Total time: 18 minutes

Servings: 2

Ingredients:

- 350 g of mixed mince
- Sweet potato fries
- ¼ medium onion, peeled and diced
- 2 tablespoons of fried onions
- 2 fried eggs
- 1 teaspoon of garlic puree
- 2 teaspoons of oregano
- 1 teaspoon of thyme
- 1 teaspoon of parsley
- ½ teaspoon of rosemary
- Salt & Pepper

Cooking Instructions:

1. Peel and dice the onion.

2. In a medium bowl, add together the mince, the garlic and the onion with the seasoning and give everything a good mix.

3. Make the mixture into hamburger shapes. Place them in your Air Fryer. Cook at 180°C/360°F for 15 minutes.

4. Serve with a fried egg, sweet potato fries and some fried onion.

Juicy Lucy Cheese Burger

Preparation time: 5 minutes

Cook time: 15 minutes

Total time: 20 minutes

Servings: 2

Ingredients:

- 250 g of minced beef
- 1 medium onion, diced
- 100 g of cheddar cheese
- 1 teaspoon of mixed herbs
- Salt & Pepper

Cooking Instructions:

1. Preheat your Air Fryer to 180°C. Dice your onion and set aside.

2. In a medium bowl, add together the onion, minced beef and seasoning and give everything a good mix. Roll them into 4 even sized balls.

3. Place them on a chopping board and cut the burgers into thin pieces. Place half of the cheese in between two of the burgers.

4. Merge the burgers together, then the cheese and then the second burger. Repeat the same procedure for the third and fourth burgers. Pinch around the sides to hide the cheese.

5. Place the 2 burgers in your Air Fryer. Cook at 180°C for 15 minutes. Remove the burgers and check to ensure that the cheese has melted in the center by putting a knife or cake tester through it.

6. If the juices run clear, it means that your burgers are cooked, if they don't, you need to add them back in the Air Fryer and cook for additional 10 minutes at 180°C.

7. Serve in a burger bun with loads of garnish.

AIR FREYR VEGAN & VEGETARIAN RECIPES

Vegetable Samosas

Preparation time: 3 minutes

Cook time: 6 minutes

Total time: 9 minutes

Servings: 12

Ingredients:

- 6 weight watchers wraps, chopped
- Egg wash
- 200 g of leftover vegetable Korma

Cooking Instructions:

1. Chop the weight watcher wraps in half with a scissors. Egg wash the inside of the wrap.

2. Place the leftover vegetable samosa filling with half of the wrap. Press down the other side with a fork. Give it a layer of egg wash.

3. Place them in your Air Fryer. Cook at 200°C/400°F for 3 minutes. Flip over with a tongs and cook for additional 3 minutes or until all the vegetable samosas are cooked.

4. Serve and enjoy!

Buffalo Cauliflower

Servings: 3 – 4

Ingredients:

- 1 medium head cauliflower, chopped into 1 1/2" florets
- 2-3 tbsp. of Frank's Red Hot Sauce
- 1 ½ tsp. of maple syrup
- 2 tsp. of avocado oil
- 2-3 tbsp. of nutritional yeast
- ¼ tsp. of sea salt
- 1 tbsp. of cornstarch or arrowroot starch

Cooking Instructions:

1. Preheat the Air Fryer to 360°F. In a medium bowl, add all of the ingredients except cauliflower.

2. Give everything good whisk to combine. Add the cauliflower and toss everything to coat evenly. Add half of your cauliflower to Air Fryer.

3. Cook them for about 12 to 14 minutes, shaking halfway, or until your desired consistency is achieved.

4. Repeat the same procedure with the rest of the cauliflower, except lower cook time to about 9 to 10 minutes.

5. Refrigerate the cauliflower in sealed bowl for at least 4 days. To reheat, add them back to your Air Fryer and cook for about 1-2 minutes, or until warmed and crispy.

6. Serve and enjoy!

Potato Chips

Ingredients:

- 1 large Russet Potato, thinly sliced
- Grapeseed Oil Cooking Spray, or any high-heat oil spray
- Pinch of sea salt

Cooking Instructions:

1. Squeeze out much of the moisture from the potato slices with a paper towel. Spray your Air Fryer basket with the oil spray.

2. Add the potatoes in a single layer inside your Air Fryer basket. Spray the tops of the potatoes with the oil spray and sprinkle with salt.

3. Cook at 450°F for about 10 to 15 minutes or until the edges of the potatoes are golden brown and crisp.

4. Remove the chips from your Air Fryer and allow them to crisp up on the cooling rack overnight.

5. Serve and enjoy!

Sticky Mushroom Rice

Preparation time: 5 minutes

Cook time: 20 minutes

Total time: 25 minutes

Servings: 6

Ingredients:

- 16 oz. of jasmine rice uncooked
- ½ cup of soy sauce or gluten free tamari
- 4 tbsp. of maple syrup
- 4 cloves garlic, finely chopped
- 2 tsp. of Chinese 5 Spice
- ½ tsp. of ground ginger
- 4 tbsp. of white wine or rice vinegar
- 16 oz. of cremini mushrooms wiped clean, cut any huge mushrooms in half
- ½ cup of peas frozen

Cooking Instructions:

1. Cook your rice according to your desired doneness. In a medium bowl, mix together the next 6 ingredients and set aside.

2. Add the mushrooms in your Air Fryer. Cook at 350°F for 10 minutes. Flip the mushrooms to cook on other side.

3. Pour the liquid mixture and peas over the top of the mushrooms and stir. Cook for additional 5 minutes at the same temperature.

4. Pour the mushroom/pea sauce over the pot of rice and give everything a good stir.

5. Serve and enjoy!

Veggie Bake Cakes

Preparation time: 2 minutes

Cook time: 12 minutes

Total time: 14 minutes

Servings: 2

Ingredients:

- Leftover vegetable bake
- 1 tablespoon of plain flour

Cooking Instructions:

1. Preheat your Air Fryer to 180°C.

2. In a medium bowl, mix together the flour with the leftover vegetable bake to form a thick dough.

3. Place the vegetable bake mixture into your Air Fryer baking mat.

4. Cook them at 180°C for 12 minutes.

5. Serve and enjoy!

Cauliflower Chickpea Tacos

Servings: 4

Prep Time 10 minutes

Cook Time 20 minutes

Total Time 30 minutes

Ingredients:

- 4 cups of cauliflower florets, cut into bite-sized pieces
- 19 ounces can of chickpeas, drained and rinsed
- 2 tbsp. of olive oil
- 2 tbsp. of taco seasoning

For Serving:

- 8 small tortillas
- 2 avocados, sliced
- 4 cups of cabbage shredded
- Coconut yogurt

Cooking Instructions:

1. Preheat your Air Fryer to 390°F/200°C.

2. In a medium bowl, add together the cauliflower and chickpeas with the olive oil and taco seasoning.

3. Place them into your Air Fryer basket. Cook for about 20 minutes, shaking the basket occasionally or until cooked through.

4. Cauliflower will be golden when fully cooked. Serve in tacos with avocado slices, cabbage and coconut yogurt.

5. Serve and enjoy!

Fried Ravioli

Ingredients:

- 1 (14 oz.) jar marinara sauce
- 1 (9 oz.) box cheese ravioli, store-bought or meat ravioli
- 1 tsp. of olive oil
- 2 cups of Italian-style bread crumbs
- 1 cup of buttermilk
- ¼ cup of Parmesan cheese

Cooking Instructions:

1. Place the ravioli in buttermilk.//
2. Add olive oil to breadcrumbs, then press the ravioli into it.
3. Place the breaded ravioli into your Air Fryer on baking paper.
4. Cook them at 200°F for about 5 minutes.
5. Serve hot with marinara sauce for dipping.

Mediterranean Vegetables

Preparation time: 5 minutes

Cook time: 20 minutes

Total time: 25 minutes

Servings: 4

Ingredients:

- 50 g of cherry tomatoes
- 1 large courgette, sliced
- 1 green pepper, sliced
- 1 large parsnip, peeled and diced
- 1 small carrot, diced
- 1 teaspoon of mixed herbs
- 2 tablespoons of honey
- 1 teaspoon of mustard
- 2 teaspoons of garlic puree
- 6 tablespoons of olive oil
- Salt & Pepper

Cooking Instructions:

1. Chop and sliced up the courgette and green pepper. Peel and dice the parsnip and carrot.

2. Add the cherry tomatoes and drizzle with 3 tbsp. of olive oil. Cook at 180°C for 15 minutes.

3. Meanwhile, mix the remaining ingredients into your Air Fryer baking dish. Place the vegetables into the baking dish when they are done cooking.

4. Shake the vegetables very well to be covered in the marinade. Sprinkle with extra salt and pepper. Cook for additional 5 minutes at 200°C.

5. Serve and enjoy!

Spicy Cauliflower Stir-Fry

Preparation time: 5 minutes

Cook time: 25 minutes

Total time: 30 minutes

Servings: 4

Ingredients:

- 1 head of cauliflower, cut into florets
- ¾ cup of onion white, sliced
- 5 cloves garlic, sliced
- 1 ½ tbsp. of tamari or gluten free tamari
- 1 tbsp. of rice vinegar
- ½ tsp. of coconut sugar
- 1 tbsp. of Sriracha or your desired hot sauce
- 2 scallions, for garnish

Cooking Instructions:

1. Add the cauliflower in your Air Fryer. Cook at 350°F for 10 minutes.

2. Remove and shake the cauliflower and add back in the compartment. Add the sliced onion, give everything a good stir.

3. Cook for additional 10 minutes. Add the garlic, stir and cook another 5 minutes.

4. In a medium bowl, mix together the soy sauce, rice vinegar, coconut sugar, Sriracha, salt & pepper.

5. Pour the mixture to cauliflower and give everything a good stir. Cook for additional 5 minutes at the same temperature.

6. Sprinkle sliced scallions over the top for garnish.

7. Serve and enjoy!

Cheesy Potato Wedges

Preparation time: 15 minutes

Cook time: 16 minutes

Total time: 31 minutes

Servings: 4

Ingredients:

For the Potatoes:

- 1 pound of fingerling potatoes
- 1 teaspoon of extra virgin olive oil
- 1 teaspoon of kosher salt
- 1 teaspoon of ground black pepper
- ½ teaspoon of garlic powder

For the Cheese Sauce:

- ½ cup of raw cashews
- ½ teaspoon of ground turmeric
- ½ teaspoon of paprika
- 2 tablespoons of nutritional yeast
- 1 teaspoon of fresh lemon juice
- 2 tbsp. to ¼ cup water

Cooking Instructions:

1. Preheat your Air Fryer for about 3 minutes at 400°F.

2. Rinse the potatoes and cut them in half lengthwise. Place the potatoes in a large bowl. Add the oil, salt, pepper, and garlic powder.

3. Toss everything to coat. Place them in your Air Fryer. Cook for about 16 minutes, shaking halfway through the cooking time.

4. In a high-speed blender, add together the cashews, turmeric, paprika, nutritional yeast, and lemon juice and blend on low.

5. Remove the cooked potatoes from the Air Fryer to a piece of parchment paper. Drizzle the cheese sauce over the potato wedges.

6. Place them pan in your Air Fryer. Cook them at 400°F for additional 2 minutes. Serve and enjoy!

Vegan Potato Latkes

Preparation time: 2 minutes

Cook time: 8 minutes

Total time: 10 minutes

Serves: 12-14

Ingredients:

- 2½ cups of peeled, shredded white potato
- ½ cup of minced sweet onion
- 3 tablespoons of arrowroot starch
- 1 prepared bob's red mill egg replacement
- ½ teaspoon of smoked paprika, optional
- ¼ teaspoon of black pepper, optional
- Applesauce, for serving

Cooking Instructions:

1. Preheat the Air Fryer to 350°F.

2. In a medium bowl, mix together the potato, onion, starch, and prepared egg.

3. Add the spices if desired. Form about 2 tbsp. of the mixture into a thick flattened disc.

4. Place them in your Air Fryer. Repeat the procedure depending on the size of your Air Fryer.

5. Cook the latkes for about 5 minutes, flip the latkes, and cook for additional 3 minutes or until golden brown and crisp.

6. Serve and enjoy!

Thai Veggie Bites

Preparation time: 5 minutes

Cook time: 20 minutes

Total time: 25 minutes

Servings: 16

Ingredients:

- 1 large broccoli
- 1 large cauliflower
- 6 large carrots
- Handful garden peas
- ½ cauliflower, made into cauliflower rice
- 1 medium onion, peeled and diced
- 1 medium courgette
- 2 leeks, rinsed and thinly sliced
- 1 can of coconut milk
- 50 g plain flour
- 1 cm cube of ginger, peeled and grated
- 1 tablespoon of garlic puree
- 1 tablespoon of olive oil
- 1 tablespoon of Thai green curry paste
- 1 tablespoon of coriander
- 1 tablespoon of mixed spice
- 1 teaspoon of cumin
- Salt & Pepper

Cooking Instructions:

1. Cook the onion with the garlic, ginger and olive oil in a wok or until the onion has soften.

2. Cook your vegetables for about 20 minutes except for the courgette and leek.

3. Add the courgette, the leek and the curry paste to your wok and cook for additional 5 minutes on a medium heat.

4. Add the coconut milk and the remaining seasoning and give everything a good mix. Add the cauliflower rice and mix well.

5. Simmer for about 10 minutes to reduce the sauce by half. Add the steamed vegetables and give everything a good mix.

6. Refrigerate for at least an hour to allow to cool. After an hour, form them into bite sizes.

7. Place them in your Air Fryer. Cook at 180°C for 10 minutes.

8. Serve with a cooling dip and enjoy!

AIR FRYER APPETIZER RECIPES

Roasted Parsnips

Preparation time: 2 minutes

Cook time: 11 minutes

Total time: 13 minutes

Servings: 4

Ingredients:

- 6 small parsnips, peeled and chopped
- Salt & Pepper

Cooking Instructions:

1. Peel and chop the parsnips diagonally to have the same shaped roasted parsnips.

2. Add the chopped parsnip into your Instant Pot steamer basket. Place the basket into your Instant Pot and place it on top of the trivet.

3. Add 1 cup of warm water over the parsnips. Close and lock the lid in place and ensure that the valve is in sealing position.

4. Select Manual, High Pressure for 3 minutes. When the timer beeps, do a quick pressure release. Carefully open the lid and transfer the parsnips to a chopping board.

5. Season with salt and pepper. Place the parsnips in your Air Fryer. Cook at 200°C/400°F for 8 minutes.

6. Serve and enjoy!

Monte Cristo Sandwich

Serves: 1

Ingredients:

- 1 egg
- 3 tbsp. of half and half
- ¼ tsp. of vanilla extract
- 2 slices sourdough, white or multigrain bread
- 2½ oz. of sliced Swiss cheese
- 2 oz. of slices deli ham
- 2 oz. of sliced deli turkey
- 1 tsp. of butter, melted
- Powdered sugar
- Raspberry jam, for serving

Cooking Instructions:

1. In a medium bowl, combine together the egg, half and half and vanilla extract. Place the bread on the counter.

2. Make a sandwich with 1 slice of Swiss cheese, ham, turkey and then a second slice of Swiss cheese on one slice of the bread.

3. Top with the other slice of bread and press down with a fork to flatten. Preheat your Air Fryer to 350°F.

4. Cut a piece of aluminum foil and brush the foil with melted butter. Dip both sides of the sandwich in the egg batter.

5. Allow the batter to soak into bread for at least 30 seconds per side. Place the sandwich on the greased aluminum foil and Place them into your Air Fryer basket.

6. Brush the top of the sandwich with melted butter. Cook at 350°F for 10 minutes. Flip the sandwich over.

7. Brush with butter and cook for another 8 minutes. Place the sandwich to a serving bowl and sprinkle with powdered sugar.

8. Serve with raspberry or blackberry preserves on the side.

Cinnamon Toast

Preparation time: 5 minutes

Cook time: 5 minutes

Total time: 10 minutes

Servings: 6

Ingredients:

- 12 slices Bread whole wheat
- 1 stick salted butter, room temperature
- ½ cup of white sugar
- 1 ½ tsp. of ground cinnamon
- 1 ½ tsp. of pure vanilla extract
- 4-6 cranks fresh ground black pepper, optional

Cooking Instructions:

1. In a medium bowl, mash the softened butter with a fork and add in sugar, cinnamon, pepper and vanilla.

2. Give everything a good stir to combine. Spread on bread, and ensure that the entire surface is completely covered.

3. Place them into your Air Fryer. Cook at 400°F for 5 minutes. Transfer them to a chopping board and cut diagonally.

4. Serve and enjoy!

Spicy Dill Pickle Fries

Preparation time: 15 minutes

Cook time: 15 minutes

Total time: 30 minutes

Servings: 12

Ingredients:

- 1 ½ (16 oz.) jars spicy dill pickle spears
- 1 cup of all-purpose flour
- ½ tsp. of paprika
- ¼ cup of milk
- 1 egg, beaten
- 1 cup of panko bread crumbs
- Cooking spray

Cooking Instructions:

1. Rinse the pickles and pat them dry with a paper towel. In a medium bowl, combine together the flour and paprika.

2. In a separate bowl, combine together the milk and beaten egg. Place the panko in a third bowl. Heat your Air Fryer to 400°F.

3. Dip a pickle first in flour mixture, then in egg mixture, and then in bread crumbs until they are well coated. Transfer the coated pickle to a plate.

4. Repeat the same procedure with remaining pickles. Spray coated pickles with cooking spray. Place them in a single layer in your Air Fryer basket.

5. Cook the pickles in batches if to avoid overcrowding the fryer. Cook for 14 minutes; flip the pickles halfway through cooking time.

6. Serve and enjoy!

Stuffed Mushrooms with Sour Cream

Preparation time: 30 minutes

Cook time: 15 minutes

Total time: 45 minutes

Ingredients:

- 24 mushrooms, caps and stems diced
- ½ orange bell pepper, diced
- ½ onion, diced
- 1 medium carrot, diced
- 2 slices of bacon, diced
- 1 cup of shredded Cheddar cheese
- ½ cup of sour cream
- 1 ½ tbsp. of shredded Cheddar cheese

Cooking Instructions:

1. Add the mushroom stems, orange bell pepper, onion, carrot, and bacon in a skillet.

2. Cook the ingredients over medium heat, stirring occasionally until softened for about 5 minutes.

3. Stir in 1 cup Cheddar cheese and sour cream. Cook the ingredients for about 2 minutes or until the cheese has melted.

4. Preheat your Air Fryer to 350°F/175°C. Place the mushroom caps on the baking tray.

5. Add stuffing in a heaped fashion to each mushroom cap. Sprinkle with 1 ½ tbsp. of Cheddar cheese on top.

6. Add the tray of mushrooms into your Air Fryer basket. Cook for about 8 minutes or until cheese melts.

7. Serve and enjoy!

Mozzarella Sticks

Preparation time: 20 minutes

Cook time: 15 minutes

Total time: 35 minutes

Servings: 4

Ingredients:

Batter:

- ½ cup of water
- ¼ cup of all-purpose flour
- 5 tbsp. of cornstarch
- 1 tbsp. of cornmeal
- 1 tsp. of garlic powder
- ½ tsp. of salt

Coating:

- 1 cup of panko bread crumbs
- ½ tsp. of salt
- ½ tsp. of ground black pepper
- ½ tsp. of parsley flakes
- ½ tsp. of garlic powder
- ¼ tsp. of onion powder
- ¼ tsp. of dried oregano
- ¼ tsp. of dried basil
- 5 oz. of mozzarella cheese, cut into 1/2-inch strips
- 1 tbsp. of all-purpose flour, or more
- Cooking spray

Cooking Instructions:

1. In a medium bowl, add the water, flour, cornstarch, cornmeal, garlic powder, and salt. Give everything a good mix into a batter.

2. Adjust ingredients if desired to suit your desired consistency. In a separate bowl, stir in panko, salt, pepper, parsley, garlic powder, onion powder, oregano, and basil.

3. Coat each mozzarella stick with flour. Dredge each stick in the batter and toss in the panko mixture until fully coated.

4. Add the sticks in a single layer on a baking sheet and refrigerate for an hour. Heat your Air Fryer to 400°F/200°C.

5. Place a row of mozzarella sticks in your Air Fryer basket and spray with a cooking spray. Cook the sticks for 6 minutes.

6. Flip the sticks with tongs when they are half way cooked. Cook for additional 7 to 9 minutes or until golden brown.

7. Serve and enjoy!

Bacon-Cheddar Stuffed Potato Skins

Yield: 2 - 4

Ingredients:

- 2 medium russet potatoes, sliced in half lengthwise
- Olive or vegetable oil
- Pinch of salt
- Freshly ground black pepper
- 2 cups of grated Cheddar cheese
- Bacon, cooked and chopped
- Scallions, chopped
- Sour cream

Cooking Instructions:

1. Preheat your Air Fryer to 400°F. Slice the potatoes in half lengthwise.

2. Rube the oil on the potatoes and season with salt and black pepper. Place the potatoes, cut side up to your Air Fryer basket.

3. Cook at 400°F for 20 minutes. Turn the potatoes over and cook at 400°F for another 10 minutes.

4. Discard the flesh out of the potato, and leave about ½-inch of the potato in the skin. Rub the inside of the potato skins with oil.

5. Season the potatoes again with salt and pepper. Cook at 400°F, skin side up, for 10 minutes. Take the grated Cheddar cheese and bacon to fill the potato skin.

6. Place the skins back to your Air Fryer basket. Cook at 360°F for 2 minutes, or until the cheese is melted.

7. Top with the chopped scallions and serve with sour cream

Tomato Basil Scallops

Preparation time: 5 minutes

Cook time: 10 minutes

Total time: 15 minutes

Servings: 2

Ingredients:

- ¾ cup of heavy whipping cream
- 1 tbsp. of tomato paste
- 1 tbsp. of chopped fresh basil
- 1 tsp. of minced garlic
- ½ tsp. of salt
- ½ tsp. of pepper
- 1 12 ounces package of frozen spinach thawed and drained
- 8 jumbo sea scallops
- Vegetable oil to spray
- More salt and pepper to season scallops

Cooking Instructions:

1. Spray a 7-inch heatproof pan with the vegetable oil.

2. Add the spinach in an even layer at the bottom. Spray each side of the scallops with vegetable oil, and sprinkle with salt and pepper.

3. Add the scallops in the pan on top of the spinach. In a medium bowl, mix together the cream, tomato paste, basil, garlic, salt and pepper.

4. Pour the mixture over the spinach and scallops. Place them in your Air Fryer. Cook at 350°F for 10 minutes or until the scallops have an internal temperature of 135°F.

5. Serve warm and enjoy!

Grilled Cheese Sandwich

Preparation time: 2 minutes

Cook time: 8 minutes

Total time: 10 minutes

Servings: 1

Ingredients:

- 2 slices of sandwich bread
- 2-3 slices of cheddar cheese
- 2 tsp. of butter or mayonnaise

Cooking Instructions:

1. Add the cheese between bread slices.
2. Butter the outside of both slices of bread.
3. Place them in your Air Fryer. Cook at 370°F for 8 minutes.
4. Turn it when they have cooked halfway through to cook on other side.
5. Serve and enjoy!

Buffalo-Ranch Chickpeas

Preparation time: 5 minutes

Cook time: 20 minutes

Total time: 25 minutes

Servings: 2

Ingredients:

- 1 (15 oz.) can chickpeas, drained and rinsed
- 2 tbsp. of Buffalo wing sauce
- 1 tbsp. of dry ranch dressing mix

Cooking Instructions:

1. Preheat your Air Fryer to 350°F/175°C. Line a baking sheet with paper towels and place the chickpeas over the paper towels.

2. Add a layer of paper towels over the chickpeas and squeeze to remove any excess moisture. Add the chickpeas in a bowl.

3. Add wing sauce to the bowl and give everything a good mix to combine. Add the ranch dressing powder and give everything a good mix.

4. Place chickpeas in your Air Fryer basket. Cook for 8 minutes. Turn the chickpeas and cook for another 5 minutes.

5. Shake the chickpeas again and cook for more 5 minutes. Shake them and cook for the last 2 minutes. Allow them to cool for about 5 minutes.

6. Serve and enjoy!

French Toast Soldiers

Preparation time: 5 minutes

Cook time: 10 minutes

Total time: 15 minutes

Servings: 2

Ingredients:

- 4 slices of whole meal bread, chopped into soldiers
- 2 large eggs
- ¼ cup of whole milk
- ¼ cup of brown sugar
- 1 tablespoon of honey
- 1 teaspoon of cinnamon
- Dash of nutmeg
- Dash of icing sugar

Cooking Instructions:

1. First, chop the slices of whole meal bread into soldiers. Each slice is expected to make 4 soldiers.

2. In a medium bowl, add the remaining ingredients except the icing sugar and give everything a good mix.

3. Dredge each soldier into the mixture to coat with the mixture. Place them into your Air Fryer.

4. Cook at 160°C for 10 minutes or until they are nice and crispy. Flip them halfway when cooking to cook on other sides.

5. Serve with a sprinkle of icing sugar and some fresh berries.

Greasy Home Fried Potatoes

Preparation time: 30 minutes

Cook time: 35 minutes

Total time: 1 hour 5 minutes

Servings: 4

Ingredients:

- 3 large Potatoes, scrubbed and diced into ½ - ¾ cubes
- 1 small yellow onion, diced
- 1 small red pepper, diced, optional
- 2 tbsp. of bacon grease (or ghee, or olive oil)
- 2 tsp. of sea salt
- 1 tsp. of onion powder
- 1 tsp. of garlic powder
- 1 tsp. of paprika

Cooking Instructions:

1. In a large bowl, add the diced potatoes and pour enough water to cover and soak for 20 to 30 minutes. Mix in all seasonings and put to one side.

2. Grease the Air Fryer basket coconut oil. Drain the potatoes, and pat dry with a paper towel. Place them potatoes in a large bowl and add bacon grease or oil.

3. Give everything a good mix and place them in your Air Fryer basket. Cook the potatoes at 370°F for 20 minutes, shaking occasionally during cooking.

4. Add the diced onion and red peppers in a medium bowl and set aside. When the potatoes are done cooking, transfer potatoes into bowl with onions/peppers.

5. Add your seasonings and give everything a good mix. Place the mixture into your Air Fryer Basket. Place them in your Air Fryer.

6. Cook at 380°F for additional 5 to 10 minutes, shaking a few times or until potatoes are browned and onions are soft.

7. Serve and enjoy!

Blooming Onion

Preparation time: 10 minutes

Cook time: 15 minutes

Total time: 25 minutes

Servings: 2

Ingredients:

- 1 large sweet onion
- ½ cup of all-purpose flour
- 1 tablespoon of seasoning salt
- 1 teaspoon of garlic powder
- ½ teaspoon of cayenne pepper
- 1 egg
- ¼ cup of milk
- Cooking spray

Cooking Instructions:

1. Cut your onion into sections to form the blooming onion petal effect. Remove the onion petals apart.

2. In a medium bowl, whisk together the flour and spices. Whisk together the egg and milk in another bowl.

3. Dredge the onion into egg mixture, cut side up and ladle the liquid over the onion to coat all of the onion pieces.

4. Dredge the onion into flour mixture, cut side up and sprinkle with flour mixture over the onion to coat each petal.

5. Shake the onion to remove any excess flour back into bowl. Spray the onion and petals with cooking spray, and ensure that each piece and section of onion is coated.

6. Place in your Air Fryer. Cook at 370°F for 10 minutes. Cook for another 5 minutes if it's not golden brown.

7. Serve and enjoy!

Sweet Potato Tots

Preparation time: 15 minutes

Cook time: 35 minutes

Total time: 50 minutes

Servings: 24

Ingredients:

- 2 sweet potatoes, peeled
- ½ tsp. of Cajun seasoning
- Olive oil cooking spray
- Sea salt

Cooking Instructions:

1. Simmer a pot of water to a boil and place the sweet potatoes.

2. Cook the potatoes for 15 minutes or until they can be pierced with a fork. Drain the potatoes and allow to cool.

3. Grate sweet potatoes into a large bowl with a box grater. Mix in Cajun seasoning and make the mixture into tot-shaped cylinders.

4. Spray your Air Fryer basket with olive oil spray. Arrange the tots in a single layer in your Air Fryer basket without touching each other or the sides of the basket.

5. Spray tots with olive oil spray and sprinkle with sea salt. Cook at 400°F/200°c for 8 minutes. Flip the tots, pray with more olive oil spray, and sprinkle with sea salt.

6. Cook for additional 8 minutes. Serve and enjoy!

Zucchini Gratin

Preparation time: 10 minutes

Cook time: 15 minutes

Total time: 25 minutes

Servings: 4

Ingredients:

- 2 zucchini, sliced
- 1 tbsp. of chopped fresh parsley
- 2 tbsp. of bread crumbs
- 4 tbsp. of grated Parmesan cheese
- 1 tbsp. of vegetable oil
- Pepper & Salt

Cooking Instructions:

1. Preheat your Air Fryer to 180°C.

2. Slice the zucchini in half lengthways and cut each of the sliced zucchini piece in half through the center.

3. Place the sliced 8 pieces of zucchini in your Air Fryer basket. In a medium bowl, add together the parsley, bread crumbs, cheese, oil and pepper to taste.

4. Cook them in two batches. Top the zucchini with the mixture. Place the Air Fryer basket and cook for 15 minutes.

5. Cook the zucchini gratin until the gratin is golden brown.

6. Serve and enjoy!

Fried Pickles

Preparation time: 10 minutes

Cook time: 20 minutes

Total time: 30 minutes

Servings: 8

Ingredients:

- ¾ cup of panko bread crumbs
- 1 teaspoon of dried oregano
- 1 teaspoon of garlic powder
- 1 teaspoon of paprika
- ½ teaspoon of salt
- ¼ teaspoon of pepper
- 1 egg
- 1 jar dill pickle slices (32 ounces)
- Ranch for dipping

Cooking Instructions:

1. Preheat your Air Fryer to 400°F. Spray your Air Fryer basket with cooking spray.

2. In a medium bowl, add together the panko, oregano, garlic powder, paprika, salt and pepper.

3. In a separate bowl, whisk egg and set aside. Rinse the pickle chips and pat dry with paper towels.

4. Dip the pickle chips first in egg and then in the breadcrumb mixture. Place them in batches, in your Air Fryer basket.

5. Cook at 400°F for 5 minutes.

6. Serve with your desired sauce and enjoy!

AIR FRYER DESSERT RECIPES

Fried Banana S'mores

Servings: 4

Ingredients:

- 4 bananas
- 3 tbsp. of mini semi-sweet chocolate chips
- 3 tbsp. of mini peanut butter chips
- 3 tbsp. of mini marshmallows
- 3 tbsp. of graham cracker cereal

Cooking Instructions:

1. Preheat your Air Fryer to 400°F. Slice into the un-peeled bananas lengthwise and slightly open the banana to form a pocket.

2. Fill each pocket on the banana with chocolate chips, peanut butter chips and marshmallows. Poke the graham cracker cereal into the filling.

3. Place them into your Air Fryer basket, standing them up. Cook at 400°F for 6 minutes, or until the banana is soft.

4. Ensure that the chocolate and marshmallows have melted and toasted. Allow them to rest for a few minutes before serving.

5. Serve and enjoy!

Apple Dumplings

Ingredients:

- 3 apples
- ½ cup of raisins
- ½ cup of brown sugar
- 2 sheets of puffed pastry (thawed)
- 2 tbsp. of butter, melted

Cooking Instructions:

1. Peel and dice your apples. In a medium bowl, mix together the brown sugar and raisins.

2. Lay out your puff pastry, and add some apples and a few tablespoons of brown sugar/raisin mixed in the center.

3. Wrap up and press the sides of the puff pastry with a fork. Brush the dough on each side with melted butter.

4. Place the pastry into a piece of foil, and wrap it up. Place them in your Air Fryer. Cook at 350°F for 15 minutes, Flip them and cook for additional 10 minutes.

5. Serve and enjoy!

Peach and Blueberry Cobbler

Preparation time: 10 minutes

Cook time: 80 minutes

Total time: 1 hour 30 minutes

Serves: 4 - 6

Ingredients:

- 1/3 cup of sugar
- 3 tbsp. of cornstarch
- Dash of salt
- 3 cups of sliced, peeled peaches (fresh or frozen and thawed)
- 2 cups of blueberries (fresh or frozen and thawed)
- Juice of ½ lemon

Topping:

- ¾ cup of all-purpose flour
- 1 tsp. of baking powder
- ¼ tsp. of salt
- 4 tbsp. of sugar
- 3 tbsp. of butter, cold
- 2/3 cup of buttermilk
- Turbinado sugar

Cooking Instructions:

1. In a medium bowl, combine together the sugar, cornstarch and a dash of salt.

2. Add the peaches, blueberries and lemon juice. Toss the fruit to coat everything with the sugar mixture.

3. Place the fruit to a 7-inch baking dish. In a separate bowl, stir together the flour, baking powder, salt and sugar.

4. Grate the butter into the flour and stir everything to coat. Stir in the buttermilk to make the dough wet. Preheat your Air Fryer to 380°F.

5. Dollop the batter over the top of the fruit, and allow some of the fruits to be uncovered. Sprinkle with the Turbinado sugar to form a crunchy texture on top of the dough.

6. Wrap the cake pan with a piece of foil, and place into your Air Fryer basket. Cook at 380°F for 65 minutes.

7. Open the basket and remove the aluminum foil. Cook at 330°F for additional 15 minutes or until the dough on top is nicely browned and the fruit is bubbling.

8. Allow the cobbler to rest for about 10 minutes before serving.

9. Serve warm with vanilla ice cream and enjoy!

Stuffed Apple Pies

Serves: 4

Ingredients:

- 4 large Granny Smith apples
- Juice of 1 lemon
- 2 Fuji or Gala apples, peeled and finely diced
- 3 tbsp. of sugar
- ¼ tsp. of ground ginger
- 1 tsp. of ground cinnamon
- Pinch of nutmeg
- 2 tbsp. of butter, cut into 4 slices
- 2 ready-made pie dough, or your homemade recipe
- 1 egg, beaten
- Coarse sanding sugar

Cooking Instructions:

1. Cut off the top of the Granny Smith apples and cut around the edge of the apple, leaving a ¼-inch border of apple next to the skin with a paring knife.

2. Use a spoon to scoop out the inside of the apple and reserve aside. Remove the core and seeds. Squeeze lemon juice on the inside of the apples.

3. Preheat your skillet over medium heat and add the butter. Cook for about 2 to 3 minutes together with the apple pulp along with the diced apples, sugar, ginger, cinnamon and nutmeg.

4. Fill the apples shells with the cooked apple mixture. Cut the pie dough into 16 strips and place 2 strips across the top of each apple.

5. Place the remaining 2 strips in the opposite direction over the apple. Brush the dough strips with the beaten egg and sprinkle the top with the sanding sugar.

6. Add the apples in your Air Fryer basket. Cook the apples at 350°F for about 10 to 12 minutes or until the crust is nicely brown and the apples have softened.

7. Serve with a scoop of ice cream or a dollop of whipped cream and enjoy!

Banana Sandwich

Preparation time: 10 minutes

Cook time: 8 minutes

Total time: 8 minutes

Serves: 2

Ingredients:

- Butter, softened
- 4 slices of white bread
- ¼ cup of chocolate hazelnut spread
- 1 banana

Cooking Instructions:

1. Preheat your Air Fryer to 370°F.

2. Lay the softened butter on one side of all the slices of bread. Add the slices of bread, buttered side down on the counter.

3. Lay the chocolate hazelnut spread on the other side of the bread slices. Use a knife to cut the banana in half and slice each half of the banana into three slices lengthwise.

4. Add the banana slices on two slices of bread and top with the rest of the slices of bread to make two sandwiches.

5. Use a knife to cut the sandwiches in half to fit into your Air Fryer basket. Place the sandwiches to your Air Fryer.

6. Cook at 370°F for 5 minutes. Flip them over and cook for additional 2 to 3 minutes, or until the top bread slices are nicely browned.

7. Allow the sandwiches to cool for a couple of minutes before serving.

8. Serve and enjoy!

Homemade Chocolate Cake

Ingredients:

- 1½ cup of flour
- ¾ cup of sugar
- 3 tbsp. of cocoa powder (unsweetened)
- 1 tsp. of baking soda
- 1 tsp. of salt
- 1 tsp. of vanilla
- ¼ cup of vegetable oil
- 1 cup of water
- Non-stick cooking spray

Cooking Instructions:

1. In a medium bowl, add together the flour, sugar, cocoa powder, baking soda, salt, vanilla extract, oil, and water.

2. Give everything a good mix. Spray your Air Fryer safe pan with non-stick cooking spray. Add the cake batter into the safe pan.

3. Place them in your Air Fryer. Cook at 330°F for 30 minutes.

4. Serve and enjoy!

Air Fryer Donuts

Ingredients:

- 1 can of biscuits
- Non-stick cooking spray
- 4 tbsp. of sugar
- 4 tbsp. of cinnamon

Cooking Instructions:

1. Open the can of biscuits and allow them to rest for about 20 minutes, to soft.

2. Blend the sugar and cinnamon on a plate. Give the mixture a good mix to form dough. Roll the dough into a ball.

3. Roll them into a long string and press the end with a fork to attach together. Roll into the sugar/cinnamon mixture.

4. Spray the dough with non-stick cooking spray. Place them in your Air Fryer basket. Cook at 390°F for 4 minutes.

5. Serve and enjoy!

Flaky Buttermilk Biscuits

Preparation time: 5 minutes

Cook time: 8 minutes

Total time: 13 minutes

Servings: 16

Ingredients:

- 530 g Self Raising flour
- 120 g of butter
- 500 ml of buttermilk
- ½ egg, beaten, optional

Cooking Instructions:

1. In a medium bowl, add the butter and flour. Rub the fat into the flour.

2. Give everything a good mix until it looks like coarse breadcrumbs. Pour in the buttermilk and give everything a good mix with a fork.

3. Use your hands to make the mixture into a dough ball. Roll out the dough and make the mixture into 16 medium sized flaky biscuits with a biscuit cutters.

4. Place about 4 of them into your Air Fryer grill pan. Cook at 180°C/360°F for 8 minutes.

5. Serve warm and enjoy!

Apple Cinnamon Empanadas

Preparation time: 15 minutes

Cook time: 18 minutes

Total time: 33 minutes

Servings: 12

Ingredients:

- 12 empanada wrappers
- 2 apples, diced
- 2 tablespoons of raw honey
- 1 teaspoon of vanilla extract
- 1 teaspoon of cinnamon
- 1/8 teaspoon of nutmeg
- 1 teaspoon of olive oil spray
- 2 teaspoons of cornstarch
- 1 teaspoon of water

Cooking Instructions:

1. Place a saucepan on medium-high heat. And place the apples, cinnamon, nutmeg, honey, and vanilla.

2. Give everything a good stir and cook for about 2 to 3 minutes or until the apples are soft. In a medium bowl, mix together the cornstarch and water.

3. Add the mixture to the pan and give everything a good stir. Cook for 30 seconds. Spread the empanada wrappers on a flat surface.

4. Place the apple mixture to each empanada. Close the empanadas and roll them in half. Pinch the crust along each of the edges.

5. Roll the empanadas sides inwards and twist the crust until closed. Add them to your Air Fryer basket.

6. Cook at 400°F for 8 minutes. Flip the empanadas and cook for another 10 minutes. Allow to cool for a couple of minutes before serving.

7. Serve and enjoy!

Mini Cherry and Cheese Streusel Tartlets

Serves: 6

Ingredients:

- 6 oz. of cream cheese, softened
- 3 tbsp. of sugar
- 1 egg
- 1 tbsp. of all-purpose flour
- ½ tsp. of vanilla extract
- 6 packaged mini graham cracker tartlet crusts
- 2 cups of cherry pie filling

Streusel Topping:

- 5 tbsp. of all-purpose flour
- 2 tbsp. of sugar
- ½ tsp. of ground cinnamon
- 1/3 cup of walnuts, chopped
- 3 tbsp. of melted butter

Cooking Instructions:

1. Preheat your Air Fryer to 330°F. In a medium bowl, combine together the cream cheese, sugar, egg, flour and vanilla extract.

2. Give everything a good mix until smooth. Add the cream cheese mixture into the bottom of the tartlet shells. Cook about three tartlets at 330°F for 4 minutes.

3. In another bowl, combine together the flour, sugar, cinnamon, walnuts and melted butter to make the streusel topping.

4. Toss everything with a fork until it forms small crumbles and put to one side. Ladle 2 tbsp. of cherry pie filling into each tartlet, on top of the cheese layer.

5. Sprinkle each one with the streusel topping. Place the tartlets back into your Air Fryer in batches. Cook at 330°F for another 15 minutes or until golden brown.

6. Serve warm with some whipped cream if desired and enjoy!

Sugared Dough Dippers with Chocolate Amaretto Sauce

Serves: 10 to 15

Ingredients:

- 1 lb. of bread dough, defrosted
- ½ cup of butter, melted
- ¾ - 1 cup sugar
- 1 cup of heavy cream
- 12 oz. of good quality semi-sweet chocolate chips
- 2 tbsp. of Amaretto liqueur (or almond extract)

Cooking Instructions:

1. Roll the dough into two 15-inch logs and cut each of the log into 20 slices with a knife.

2. Cut each slice of the dough in half and twist the dough together into halves for about 3 to 4 times.

3. Add the twisted dough on a cookie sheet, brush the sides with melted butter and sprinkle the dough twists with sugar.

4. Preheat your Air Fryer to 350°F and brush the bottom of your Air Fryer basket with melted butter. Cook the dough twists in batches.

5. Cook about 8 to 12 doughs in your Air Fryer basket or depending on the size of your basket. Cook for about 5 minutes.

6. Flip the dough strips over and brush the other side with butter. Cook for another 3 minutes. Meanwhile, make the chocolate amaretto sauce.

7. Simmer heavy cream over medium heat. In a large bowl, add together the chocolate chips and pour the hot cream over the chocolate chips.

8. Give everything a good stir until the chocolate begins to melt. Give everything a good whisk until the chocolate is melted and the sauce is smooth.

9. Stir in the Amaretto and transfer to a serving bowl. Transfer the batches of dough twists in a shallow dish when you are done cooking.

10. Brush them with melted butter and sprinkle with sugar, shaking the dish to cover both sides. Serve with the warm chocolate Amaretto sauce on the side and enjoy!

Steak French Fries

Ingredients:

- 3 large russet potatoes, cut into large wedges
- 2 tbsp. of oil

Cooking Instructions:

1. Cut your potatoes into large wedges, that resembles French fries.

2. In a large bowl, add all of the cut French fries, add 2 tbsp. of oil, and give everything a good mix.

3. Spread them out in your Air Fryer basket. Cook at 400°F for 12 minutes. Flip them when they are half way cooked.

4. Cook them for additional 10 minutes at the same temperature. Transfer them to a bowl and season with salt.

5. Serve and enjoy!

Apple Fries with Caramel Cream Dip

Serves: 8 - 10

Ingredients:

- 3 Pink Lady or Honeycrisp apples, peeled, cored and cut into 8 wedges
- ½ cup of flour
- 3 eggs, beaten
- 1 cup of graham cracker crumbs
- ¼ cup of sugar
- 8 ounces whipped cream cheese
- ½ cup caramel sauce, plus more for garnish

Cooking Instructions:

1. In a medium bowl, toss the apple slices and flour. Make your working station.

2. Beat the eggs in a medium bowl, and combining the crushed graham crackers and sugar in a separate bowl.

3. Dredge each apple slice into the egg, and then into the graham cracker crumbs. Coat the slices on both sides and add the coated slices on a cookie sheet.

4. Preheat your Air Fryer to 380°F. Spray the bottom of your Air Fryer basket with oil. Cook the apples in batches.

5. Add 1 layer of apple slices in your Air Fryer basket and spray with oil. Cook for 5 minutes, flip the apples and cook for another 2 minutes.

6. Meanwhile, make the caramel cream dip. In a separate bowl, combine together the whipped cream cheese and caramel sauce, and give everything a good mix.

7. Place the Caramel Cream Dip into a serving plate and drizzle with more caramel sauce over the top.

8. Serve warm with the caramel cream dip on the side and enjoy!

Homemade Vanilla Bean Cake

Ingredients:

- 1½ cup of flour
- ¾ cup of sugar
- 1 tsp. of baking soda
- 1 tsp. of salt
- 1 tsp. of vanilla
- ¼ cup of vegetable oil
- 1 cup of water
- Non-stick cooking spray

Cooking Instructions:

1. In a medium bowl, add together the flour, sugar, baking soda, salt, vanilla extract, oil, water.

2. Give everything a good mix. Spray your Air Fryer safe pan with non-stick cooking spray.

3. Add the cake batter into the safe pan and place them in your Air Fryer. Cook at 330°F for 30 minutes.

4. Serve and enjoy!

www.ingramcontent.com/pod-product-compliance
Lightning Source LLC
Chambersburg PA
CBHW082028120526
44592CB00038B/2301